CW00806550

Common Sayings, Words and Customs; Their Origin and History

N° 1'J
___
/5°

COMMON SAYINGS,

WORDS, AND CUSTOMS:

Their Origin and History.

SELECTED BY

HENRY JAMES LOARING,

AUTHOR OF "SIGNS—THEIR ANTIQUITY AND DERIVATION,"
ETC., ETC.

PHILADELPHIA:

PORTER & COATES,

822 CHESTNUT STREET.

PREFACE.

———

A SMALL book like the present requires but a brief introduction.

It is the duty of every individual to do *something*, however trifling, towards the advancement of knowledge, which has been justly termed "The fruit of mental labour, the food and feast of the soul." To effectually accomplish this, is to direct the mind into proper channels, and call attention to those objects which tend to the gratification of curiosity. All pretensions to originality are disclaimed, the grand object having been to condense and simplify such useful and interesting facts as are likely to adhere to the memory. With this impression, and a desire that it may be of some little service, this unassuming manual is most respectfully submitted to public notice.

It only remains for the author to say, that this work has been compiled from original sources, no reference having been made to any work of a similar nature which may have appeared within the last few years.

Common Sayings.

—o—

A.

ABINGDON LAW. In the civil war of Charles I., Lords Essex and Waller held Abingdon, in Berks, against the gallant but unfortunate Prince Rupert. On that occasion the defenders put all Irish prisoners to death without trial. Hence the term "Abingdon law."

ABSENTEE TAX. This was a tax of four shillings in the pound, levied in Ireland, in 1715, on the incomes and pensions of absentees—persons who derive their incomes from one country and spend it in another—but the tax was repealed in 1753.

ADAMANT. The hardest gem, or stone, that has ever been discovered is the diamond, which the ancients called adamant, from whence arose the observation, "as hard as adamant." The diamond has also the singular property that it can only be cut by its own substance.

ADMIRAL. An admiral is a superior naval officer. The word is supposed to be derived from the Arabic *amir*, or *emir*, a commander of rank. Formerly there was a lord high admiral of England, but now that office is committed to a number of commissioners. A vice-admiral commands the second squadron, and the rear-admiral commands the third division. The admiral carries his flag at the main; the

B   I

vice-admiral at the fore ; and the rear-admiral at the mizen.
The admiral ranks with a general in the army.

ÆOLIAN HARP. This instrument consists of a long
narrow box of very thin pine, about six inches deep,
with a circle in the middle of the upper side, of an inch
and a half in diameter, in which are drilled small holes.
On this side seven, ten, or more strings of very fine cat-
gut are stretched over bridges at each end, like the bridge
of a fiddle, and screwed up or relaxed with screw-pins.
The strings must all be tuned to one and the same note
(D is, perhaps, the best), and the instrument should be
placed in a window, in which the width is exactly equal
to the length of the harp, with the sash just raised to
give the air admission When the air blows upon these
strings, with different degrees of force, it will excite different tones of sound. Sometimes the blast brings out
all the tones in full concert, at others it sinks them to
the softest murmurs. A colossal imitation of the instrument
just described was invented at Milan, in 1786, by the
Abbé Gattoni. He stretched seven strong iron wires,
tuned to the notes of the gamut, from the top of a tower
sixty feet high, to the house of a Signor Moscate, who was
interested in the success of the experiment; and this
apparatus, called the "giant's harp," in blowing weather
yielded lengthened peals of harmonious music. In a storm
this music was sometimes heard at the distance of several
miles.

AGAPÆ. Love feasts, or feasts of charity, among the
primitive Christians, at which liberal collections were made
for the poor. These feasts were held at first without scandal,
but afterwards being abused, they were condemned at the

2

Council of Carthage, A.D. 397. St. Chrysostom gives the following account of this observance, which he derives from the apostolical practice. He says, " The first Christians had all things in common, as we read in the Acts of the Apostles ; but when that equality of possessions ceased, as it did, even in the apostles' time, the Agape, or love-feast, was substituted in the room of it." Upon certain days, after partaking of the Lord's Supper, they met at a common feast, the rich bringing provisions, and the poor, who had nothing, being invited.

AGAPEMONE, or *Abode of Love*. The residence of an extraordinary sect, near Bridgewater in Somersetshire. This sect originated with Henry James Prince, an ex-clergyman of the Church of England, who claimed the attributes of Omnipotence, and obtained a wonderful in-fluence over his followers. They profess to live in a state of brotherly love, and to give themselves up to innocent amusements, not troubling about ordinary mortal affairs, but living in communion with God. Many disclosures relating to this sect have been made in the law courts in 1850, 1858, and 1860.

ALBUMS. The first album, consisting of fragments written by various persons in a blank book, is said to have been kept on the Alps, in the monastery of St. Bruno. In this every traveller, at his departure, was asked to in-scribe his name, and he usually added to it a few sentences of devotion, of thankfulness to his hosts, or of admiration of the scene around him.

ALDERMAN. This term is derived from the Saxon " ælder-man," formerly the second in rank of nobility among our Saxon ancestors, equal to the "earl" of Dano-Saxon. There were also several magistrates who bore the title of Alderman ; and the *Aldermanus totius Angliæ* seems to have been the same officer who was afterwards styled *Capitalis Justiciarius Anglice,* or Chief Justice of England.

ALEXANDRINE VERSE. About the ninth century Latin ceased to be spoken in France, and was succeeded by a mixture of Frank and bad Latin, termed the Romance tongue. The second poem published in this tongue was called "The Romance of Alexander the Great," and composed by four authors ; one of whom—the most celebrated—was Alexander of Paris. Before this time all romances were composed of eight syllables ; but, in the piece just named, the authors used verses of twelve syllables. This was the origin of the term Alexandrine verses, either from the subject of the title, or from Alexander, the French poet. (See *Romance.*)

ALLHALLOWS' EVE, or Hallow E'en, the vigil of All Saints' day, on which, formerly, many curious customs were observed, such as determining the figure and size of husbands, and other superstitions connected with a desire to pry into futurity. Some of these customs are not wholly extinct.

ALL MY EYE AND BETTY MARTIN. Many of our most popular vulgarisms have their origin in some whimsical perversion of language or of fact. St. Martin is one of the saints of the Romish Calendar, and a form of prayer to him commences with the words, " *Ora, mihi beate Martine*" (that is, " O, blessed Martin, pray for me "), &c., which, through some person who was more prone to

4

punning than praying, furnished the plebeian phrase so well known in modern slang language.

ALUMINIUM. This is a recently discovered metal, remarkable for its lightness, its silvery metallic lustre, its pure sound when struck, and its ductility, which is equal to that of copper. It is found in London clay; and but for its extreme reluctance to separate from its compounds, would be the most abundant of all metals.

AMBER. A bituminous substance, the origin of which has in vain been sought for both by ancients and moderns. Thales, one of the Greek philosophers, first noticed its property of attracting light substances, such as straws, hairs, etc., and for this reason attributed to it a certain kind of life. Amber was formerly considered to possess many medicinal virtues, and was held in high estimation by the Romans, who made it into bracelets, necklaces, and other articles of female ornament. It was termed in Greek, *electron*, whence the modern term "electricity" is derived. It is curious that, on account of its highly electrical properties, those who manufacture it are liable to violent diseases of the nerves.

AMBERGRIS, or Grey Amber. This is a perfume found in the intestines of the spermaceti whale, or floating on the sea; it is an unctuous solid body, of an ash colour. The Europeans value it only as a scent; the Asiatics and Africans use it in cookery.

AMEN. This word, so often used in Scripture, has not always the same signification. In the Hebrew it means true, faithful, certain. At the end of a prayer it implies So be it; or, So let it be; at the end of a creed, So it is.

5

It has been generally used by Jews and Christians at the conclusion of prayer.

ANCHORS.   Some ascribe the invention of anchors to the Tyrrhenians ; others to Midas, the son of Gordius.   The most ancient are said to have been of stone, and sometimes of wood, to which a great quantity of lead was usually fixed. In some places baskets full of stones, and sacks filled with sand, were employed for the same use.   All these were let down by cords into the sea, and by their weight stayed the course of the ship.   Afterwards, anchors were made of iron, at first with only one fluke, but in a short time a second was added by Eupalamus, or Anacharsis, the Scythian philosopher.

ANCIENT READING.   Originally the letters in books were only divided into lines, then into separate words, which, by degrees, were noted with accents, and distributed, by points and stops, into periods, paragraphs, chapters, and other divisions.   In some countries, as among the Orientals, the lines began from the right, and ran to the left; in others, as in northern and western nations, from the left to the right.   In the Chinese books, the lines read from top to bottom.   The Grecians followed both directions alternately, going in the one and returning in the other, called *boustrophedon*, which is derived from the Greek, signifying "bullock" and "I turn," like the furrows in ploughing.   The end of the book, now denoted by *finis*, was anciently marked with a <, called *coronis*.   There also occur certain formulæ at the beginning and end of books, exhorting the reader to be courageous, and proceed to the following volume.   This was common among the Jews. The Mahometans place the name of God at the beginning of all their books, which cannot fail to procure them protection, on account of the infinite regard paid to that name. (See *Books.*)

ANCIENTS. Barristers were at one time called apprentices of the law, from *apprendre*, to learn. Above them formerly were the "ancients." This was a degree of precedence bestowed as a mark of honour upon barristers, though enjoyed as a right by the sons of judges. Among the lawyers in the Temple, such as have passed their reading are called ancients ; and in Gray's Inn, the four classes that compose the Society consist of ancients, barristers, benchers, and students.

ANIMALS. Ancient annalists have preserved to us fewer data respecting the introduction of domestic animals into new countries, than respecting the transplantation of domestic vegetables. The camel was not employed by the Egyptians until a comparatively late period in their history ; it was unknown to the Carthaginians until after the downfall of their commonwealth ; and its first appearance in Western Africa is more recent still. America has no domestic quadruped but a species of dog, the llama tribe, and, to a certain extent, the bison or buffalo. It owes the introduction of the horse, ass, ox, sheep, goat, and the swine, as does also Australia, to European colonisation. The reindeer was successfully introduced into Iceland about a century and a quarter ago, while attempts failed, about the same time, in Scotland. The Cashmere or Thibet goat was brought to France over a generation since. The same, or an allied species, and the Asiatic buffalo, were carried to South Carolina about the year 1860. The yak, or Tartar ox, seems to thrive in France. Britain formerly nourished a vast number of wild animals, such as bears, wolves, wild

7

boars, stags, roebucks, wild bulls, etc.; but now we possess only the fox, wild cat, badger, marten, otter, weasel, hedgehog, haie, rabbit, stag, fallow deer, squirrel, dormouse, mole, and several sorts of rats and mice.

ANTŒCI, Ascii, Amphiscii, Heteroscii, Periscii, and Antipodes. These words are from the Greek; the first are those who live in the same degree of longitude, and equal opposite latitudes. The Ascii are those who have no shadow at noon, and must of course be confined to those living within the torrid zone, where the sun is vertical. Amphiscii are those who live near, or on, the equator, and cast their shadows sometimes northward, and sometimes southward. Heteroscii are those whose shadows at noon are always projected one way, and which are always opposite the sun. Periscii are those whose shadows move in a circular direction quite round them, and are confined to the inhabitants of the frigid zones, where the sun does not set for a considerable time. Antipodes are those in equal opposite latitude and longitude, and whose days and nights are directly opposite to each other; thus the inhabitants of New Zealand are the antipodes to England.

APOCRYPHA. Is derived from a Greek word, and implies something secret or not well known; but when applied to books, it denotes that their authors are not known with certainty; consequently, as their authority and genuineness are doubtful, they are not admitted as canonical. A portion of the Apocrypha is, however, allowed, and occasionally read in Catholic churches, by which it evidently appears that the Christians considered the various histories contained in it to be founded in truth; and in the year 400,

8

at the Council of Carthage, the books of Esdras and others were ordered to be read.

APOSTLES. The twelve apostles, and the mode of their deaths is thus surmised :—*Simon Peter*, a fisherman in Galilee, became a disciple of Christ, in consequence of the miraculous draught of fishes. By order of the cruel Nero, he was crucified with his head downwards, on the top of Mount Vatican. *St. Andrew* was the younger brother of St. Peter, and was first a disciple of John the Baptist. He preached the gospel through Scythia, and was crucified at Patrae, being first scourged, and then fastened to a cross formed like the letter X, with cords instead of nails, in which state of agony he remained two days. Hence the letter X is called St. Andrew's cross. *St. James*, son of Zebedee, a fisherman, was condemned to death by Herod ; the principal witness against him was overcome by remorse, and embraced Christianity, when he also was decapitated. *St. John*, his brother, is described with the Evangelists. *Philip* was also a fisherman, and preached the gospel in Upper Asia, and having exasperated the magistrates by destroying a large dragon which they worshipped, he was publicly scourged, and afterwards hung by the neck to a pillar till he died. *St. James* was, it is asserted, the son of Joseph, the reputed father of Christ, by a former wife ; and, whilst preaching at Jerusalem, was pushed headlong from the eminence on which he stood, and then stoned ; but his death blow was from the club of one Simon, a fuller. *St. Bartholomew* was also called Nathanael, and was a fisherman. This holy man was seized whilst preaching in Armenia, and either crucified with his head downwards, or, more probably, flayed alive, as this custom prevailed in the East. *St. Thomas* was a fisherman

9

of Galilee, and was termed, at one time, the incredulous disciple. He preached through India; and whilst engaged at his devotions, was stoned by order of the Brahmins, and then pierced with a lance. *St. Matthew* is described as one of the Evangelists. *St. Simon,* and *St. Jude,* or Thaddeus, suffered martyrdom by crucifixion, in Persia, where they preached the gospel. And *Judas Iscariot* destroyed himself, after having betrayed his Lord and Master to the Jews for thirty pieces of silver. (See *Evangelists.*)

APRIL FOOL DAY As the 1st of April is generally termed, is a corruption of Auld or All-Fool's Day, and originated with the Romans, who called it "Fool's Holiday," by way of ridiculing the ceremonies of the Druids. Some authors consider that it was designed to commemorate the Passion of our Saviour, which took place about that time; and as the Jews sent him backward and forward from Annas to Caiaphas, from Pilate to Herod, and afterwards back again to Pilate, that ridiculous custom was meant to mock and torment him. In the present age, persons are often sent from one place to another, in order to promote ridicule and laughter. The year formerly began on the 25th of March, and great festivals were usually kept up eight days, of which the first and last were the principal, consequently the first of April is an octave of the 25th of March. One of the best tricks in connection with this day is that of Rabelais, who being at Marseilles, without money, and desirous of going to Paris, filled some vials with brick-dust or ashes, labelled them as containing poison for the royal family of France, and put them where he knew they would be discovered. The bait took, and he was conveyed as a traitor to the capital, where the discovery of the jest occasioned universal mirth.

10

ARCHDEACON. An archdeacon is next in degree to a dean, and is a kind of subordinate bishop, with authority or jurisdiction over the clergy; and is obliged, by virtue of his office, to visit every two years in three the various churches, and see that everything is in proper repair, etc., reform abuses, and punish offenders by spiritual censure. He has power also to suspend a clergyman who acts improperly, and even to excommunicate, but the most weighty affairs are generally transferred to the bishops.

ARCHERY. The archery of England, by which, nearly to the close of the seventeenth century, her greatest battle-fields have been won, is a discovery dating back from William the Conqueror. It was during the struggle between Charles I. and his parliament, that our chronicles made their latest allusion to this grand old historic weapon. Bows were found on board that redoubtable man-of-war, the *Mary Rose,* sunk in an action with a French squadron at Spithead, in the time of Henry VIII., and one or two of those very rare specimens of old English missile weapons, found in the vessel's arm-chest by the divers employed to remove her timbers, are now preserved amongst the curiosities of the Tower and of the United Service Museum.

ARGONAUTIC EXPEDITION. This is one of the primary mythological subjects. It originated in the desire of obtaining the golden fleece, or to be more explicit, the skin of a golden ram, which had been offered to Jupiter, and kept at Colchis. To achieve this, several Grecian heroes sailed for that place, in a vessel named the *Argo,* which was the first of any consequence that sailed from Greece. But to divest the subject of fable, Jason, a chief of great valour and fortitude, sailed to Colchis, to establish a prosperous commerce. In this expedition, they met many obstacles from the rude and barbarous manners of the people whom they had to deal with; but at last they accomplished their wishes, to the fullest extent, and returned to their native country crowned with every success that could have been desired.

ARITHMETICAL CHARACTERS. The numerical characters of the ancients were composed of the letters of their alphabet. Thus, with the Romans, M stood for 1,000, D for 500, G for 100, etc. The numerical character now commonly used in Europe is the Arabic, so named from the Arabian astronomers. It is generally admitted that these symbols were introduced into Europe by the Moors, during their occupation of Spain; but there seems to be some uncertainty as to the period when they became known in France and the neighbouring countries.

ARMS Coats of arms were known in the time of Richard I., and hereditary in families about 1192, although some trace it higher, and think that it originated with the primitive people painting their bodies with various figures, to distinguish them from each other. In the time of the crusades, the knights painted their banners with different figures, for better recognition. The lions in the English arms were originally leopards, as found in an old record of 1252. Formerly, none but the nobility bore arms; but the French monarch, Charles XV., having ennobled some Parisians in the thirteenth century, the custom was adopted by other nations. Crest implies the most elevated part of the head armour, and took its origin from *crista*, a cock's comb, the cock being an emblematic figure of undaunted bravery.

12

COMMON SAYINGS.   [Ash W

ARMY. The grades are thus defined. A general is commander of an army; a lieutenant-general, second in rank to a general, commands an army in the absence of the general; major-general, an officer who commands a division, or number of regiments, next in rank below a lieutenant-general; brigadier, an officer who commands a brigade—a division of the army consisting of several squadrons of horse, or battalions of infantry,—next in command to a major-general, colonel, the chief commander in a regiment, whether infantry or cavalry (this rank is sometimes honorary, only with salary attached); lieutenant-colonel, second officer in a regiment, commanding in the absence of the colonel; major, next in rank to a lieutenant-colonel, and commanding in his absence, next in rank above a captain; adjutant, an officer whose duty it is to assist the major, receiving messages from him and conveying them to the sergeants of the companies; an aide-de-camp is an officer who attends the general to receive his orders, and carry them as directed; a captain is the commander and chief of a company of foot, or a troop of horse or dragoons; a lieutenant is next in command to a captain, and does his duty when absent, a cornet is the third officer in a troop of horse or dragoons; an ensign is the third officer in a company of foot soldiers, and carries the flag or colours; and a quartermaster has to look out for the accommodation of the men.

ASCENSION DAY. A festival held on Holy Thursday. From the earliest times this day was set apart to commemorate our Saviour's ascension into heaven All processions on this and the preceding rogation days were abolished at the Reformation.

ASH WEDNESDAY. So called from a custom in

13

the ancient Church, for penitents to appear before the bishops, clad in sackcloth, with naked feet; the priest would then put consecrated ashes of palms on their heads, emblematic of man's mortality; they were then subjected to punishment according to the extent of their transgressions, and afterwards admonished as to their future conduct.

ASPEN. A legend says that Christ, visiting the sick, passed through a wood where all the trees bowed their heads in reverence to Him. One tree alone stubbornly refused to bend, and that was the aspen. Hence a curse was uttered against it, that it should thenceforward quiver with all its leaves, and that even in the mildest weather its foliage should not be still.

ASTROLOGY This was considered by the Egyptians, Greeks, and Chaldeans, as one of their principal arts or sciences. The professors of this art pretend to foretell events, to calculate what must happen to persons in the course of their lives, etc., by observing the influence of the stars or planets at the time of their birth. Pharaoh, Nebuchadnezzar, Nero, Cæsar, Pompey, and many others had faith in this art, but they were unhappy and their end calamitous. If it were founded in truth, all who were born at the same time as the monarch would be kings or queens, and Esau and Jacob have been of the same disposition and character; and all who perish in a battle must have been born under the same planet.

ASYMPTOTES. These are right lines which approach nearer and nearer to some curve, but which, if extended for ever, would never meet.

ATLANTIC OCEAN. So called from the Atlas

14

,

Mountains in Africa, and the mythological account of Atlas carrying the world on his back. (See *Atlas.*)

ATLAS. According to heathen mythology, was king of Mauritania, in the north of Africa, possessing a thousand flocks of every kind, who in consequence of his inhospitality to Perseus, was changed into the mountain which bears his name. From its immense height, the ancients supposed that the heavens rested on its summit, and Atlas supported the world on his shoulders. This fable had its origin, it is said, from the fondness he displayed for astronomy, which he generally studied on the most elevated places, the more distinctly to observe the motions of the heavenly bodies, etc.

ATTORNEY. Attorneys are gentlemen who are sworn into the several courts of law, and are authorised to act either for plaintiff or defendant; these are often called solicitors; but properly speaking, a solicitor is an attorney who practises in Chancery cases.

AURORA BOREALIS, or northern dawn, is an electrical phenomenon. It is a lambent or flashing light seen at night; the strongest and most frequent about the Arctic circle, and the height is rarely above six or seven miles. It often darts below the clouds, and at very short distances from the earth's surface, and is even acted upon by the winds.

AUTOMATONS. Some wonderful accounts are handed down of mechanism so constructed as to resemble animals, and even human beings, in figure, and to imitate their actions. Archytas, of Tarentum, about 400 years before the Christian era, is said to have made a wooden pigeon that could fly.

15

Albertus Magnus constructed an automaton to open the door when any one knocked. The celebrated Regiomontanus made a wooden eagle that flew forth from the city, saluted the emperor, and returned. He also constructed an iron fly, which flew out of his hand and returned, after moving about the room. In 1738 an automaton flute-player was exhibited at Paris that could play in the same manner as a living performer. In 1741 Vaucanson produced a flageolet-player, which played with the left hand, and beat a tambourine with the right. He also made a duck, which dabbled in the water, swam, drank, and quacked like a real bird. A Frenchman also exhibited one a few years ago which went through some of the same movements. Automatons have been constructed which wrote, played on the pianoforte, counted, etc. During the present century a Swiss, named Mailardes, constructed a figure representing a female, which performed eighteen tunes on the piano, and continued in motion an hour. He also made another figure, representing a boy, that could write and draw.

AVE MARIA. This means "Hail, Mary!" It is generally understood as referring to a well-known prayer to the Virgin Mary, beginning with these words.

B.

BADGE OF POVERTY. About the year 1693, an Act was passed, requiring that all persons in receipt of parochial relief should wear a badge bearing a large Roman P, together with the first letter of the name of the parish or place to which they belonged, cut either in red or blue cloth, upon the shoulder of the right sleeve of the coat. This rigorous statute was repealed by George III.

BADDELEY NIGHT. Baddeley, the comic actor, in his will, left a twelfth-cake and wine for the performers of Drury Lane theatre, of which they partook every twelfth-night in the green-room, and drank to the memory of the donor. He had been cook to Foote, in whose service he imbibed a taste for the drama.

BAGPIPE. The bagpipe is almost universal throughout Asia, though at present not so much in use as it seems to have been in former ages. The earliest evidence which we have of its existence in Asia is a representation dating before the Christian era. This curious relic was discovered in the ruins of Tarsus, Cilicia. A Hindoo bagpipe, called *titty*, brought from Coimbatoor, may be seen in the East India Museum. It is in use among the Chinese musicians of Maimatchin, and met with in Persia, where it is called *nei ambánah* (from *nei*, a reed or pipe, and *ambánah*, a bag), and where also, it appears to have been more general in former ages than at present. The same may be said of the Egyptian bagpipe, *zouqqarah*, which is now of but rare occurrence. The Romans were acquainted with this instrument, and most likely the Greeks also.

BALLADS. Plutarch mentions prophetic ballads, sold to servants and silly women. Street singing was common in the Anglo-Saxon era, and the itinerants used to stand at the end of bridges, like the Roman beggars. Our ancient ballad singers sang to a fiddle, upon a barrel head and benches; at taverns, on stools; and attended wakes and fairs. Cromwell prohibited ballads. They were, till the beginning of the seventeenth century, printed in black letter, set to old and well known tunes, and chiefly sold on stalls. (See *Carols.*)

BANKS. They were first known in Italy, where the Lombard Jews kept benches in the market-place, for the exchange of money and bills. The Italian word *banco* means bench, from which bank took its origin ; and the word bankrupt is supposed to be derived from the French *banqueroute,* which signifies a breaking or failing in business ; for when a money changer became insolvent, his bench was broken, to warn the public that he could no longer continue his business.

BAPTISM. Some authors are inclined to think that baptism was instituted immediately after the deluge, in memory of the world having been purged by water. Others consider that it was added to the Jewish custom of circumcision, as a mark of distinction among the sceptical Jews ; indeed, it is well known that they practised this ceremony long before the time of Christ. The real meaning of the word is dipping or plunging ; and in the eastern Churches children are regularly immersed in water. In Milan the head of the child is plunged three times into the water, emblematic of the triune Godhead, or of the Saviour lying three days in the grave. It was formerly supposed that baptism washed away all the previous sins, and that as adults only were to be admitted to this ceremony, there was no atonement for sins subsequently committed, in consequence of which many deferred this ceremony to the latest period of their existence.

BARBER'S POLE. Different opinions have been given on this subject ; some people imagine that it is emblematic of the poll of the head, others say, and with every appearance of credit, that originally the barber's company, being incorporated with that of the surgeons,

18

was deemed equally respectable, and barbers permitted to exercise the art of phlebotomy. The pole being streaked or embellished with different coloured paint, implied that the person who could shave and cut hair, would also bleed, if necessary ; and the white streaks were intended to represent the filament which bound the arm. Barbers were separated from the surgeons, after a severe struggle for their rights, in 1744, since which they have lost the privilege of bleeding—except by a slip of the razor.

BARDS. A bard is described as a poet and a singer among the ancient Celts, whose occupation was to compose and sing verses in honour of the achievements of princes and brave men. Bards were considered the historians of their time, and dressed in blue, as an emblem of truth, similar to the primitive priests The Welsh name is *bardd,* signifying a priest, philosopher, or preacher.

BARON is a French word, denoting a degree of nobility below that of a viscount. Bracton, an ancient writer, says barons were called *Barones quasi robur belli.* This signification seems to agree with other nations, where *baroniæ* are as much as *provinciæ,* so that barons seem also originally to have had the government of territories or provinces. The origin and antiquity of baronies have occasioned laborious enquiries among English antiquaries. The most probable opinion seems to be that they were the same with our present lords of manors, to which the name of Court Baron gives some countenance. Camden refers the origin of barons by writ to Henry III., and barons by letters patent, or creation, to the 11th of Richard II. There are now no feudal baronies ; but the bishops are called by writ, and sit in the House of Lords as barons, by succession. In former

times, before there was a lord mayor in London, the bur-
gesses were called barons, as appears by the city seal and
their ancient charters. The earls palatine and marches
of England had anciently their barons under them; but no
barons, save those who held immediately of the king, were
peers of the realm. Baronets were first created by James I.
22nd May, 1611.

BARROWS. It is supposed that these hillocks or
mounds were repositories for the dead during the time
that the Romans, Saxons, etc., held the sovereignty of
England; for, on being dug into, they have been found
to contain calcined earth, burnt bones. ashes, etc In some
of them, entire stone coffins, containing skeletons, have
been found; but these in general are too short to admit a
full length body. The skeletons, therefore, lay with the
legs doubled up, and the knees pressed on the breast.
Many curiosities, such as coins, warlike instruments, urns,
armour, etc , have also been dug from them.

BATCHELOR. Anciently this name was given to
persons superior in quality to esquires, but who had not
a number of vassals sufficient to carry their banner before
them in the field of battle It was also a title given to
young knights, who, having made their first campaign,
received the military girdle. It was likewise used to deno-
minate one who had overcome another in combat the first
time he engaged in fight. The word, as describing in
modern times an unmarried man, is derived from an old
French word, which was applied either to a young man or
young woman, and in this sense was even used formerly in
the English tongue.

20

BAWTRY (Saddler of). The origin of the proverb that "the saddler of Bawtry was hanged for leaving his liquor," is thus explained. It was anciently a custom to present to malefactors, on their way to the gallows, a large bowl of ale, as the last refreshment they might ever enjoy. And a man, by trade a saddler, who was about to be executed at York, would have been saved had he stopped to drink his ale, as his reprieve was on the road, and arrived a few minutes too late.

BEARD (Blue). Gilles de Lavel, Lord of Retz, and of many other baronies and lordships in Brittany and other parts of the kingdom, one of the richest men of his day in the time of Charles VII., was burnt alive in the meadows before Nantes, 23rd December, 1440. He was the original of "Blue Beard," having murdered several wives and above 100 children; "and," as he haughtily said, "committed crimes enough to condemn to death ten thousand men."

BEARING OFF THE BELL. This phrase has its origin in horse-racing, which was introduced by the Greeks at their Olympic games, and followed by the Romans in their sports in the circle. Henry II. introduced this pastime into England, and James I. established a race-course at Croydon, as did also Charles I. at Hyde Park and Newmarket, where the horses ran for sums of money, or gold and silver bells. Hence arose the phrase above named.

BECK. This word is common in the north of England, and means a small brook, stream, or rivulet. It is found in the names of towns situated near streams, as Welbeck; but is more frequent on the Continent, as Geissbach, etc. The German word *bach* has the same meaning. *Hell-beck* is

21

from the Anglo-Saxon, and connected with the German *hell* signifies "bright," or "clear."

BEEF-EATERS. This is a corruption of the French word *beaufetiers*, or keepers of the king's plate on the side-board; and as the yeomen-of-the-guard, when in the sovereign's presence, are stationed near the beaufet, they are termed *beaufetiers*, hence beef-eaters.

BELLES LETTRES. This is merely the French appellation for polite learning, or superior subjects of education. Under this head are comprised, grammar, logic, rhetoric, poetry, music, and mathematics.

BELLS Little bells of pure gold were used in the time of Moses by the Israelites in their religious ceremonies, as we read in Exodus, 39th chapter The Jews, Greeks, and Romans, made them of brass and iron, not for the purposes of religion, but to summon people to the baths. They were introduced into this country about 550 They were formerly baptized or consecrated by the bishop; hence the name *Tom* was given to some of the largest, as the great "Tom of Oxford," in honour of Thomas à Becket. By being anointed or exorcised, ignorant people supposed that they would drive away evil spirits, chase the devil from the air, calm tempests, extinguish fire, and protect the dead. Prior to the invention of bells, people were summoned to their devotion by the noise of rattles, similar to those used by our police.

BELLS (Tolling). This had its origin in superstition, and was supposed to be an effectual plan to drive away evil spirits which haunted the house and bed of their victims

It was also intended to invite passers-by to pray for the soul of the departed.

BENEFIT OF CLERGY. This term originally meant, to exempt a clergyman from being tried for offences by laical judges ; and even if he had committed some extraordinary crime, his punishment was lighter than death.   In the dark age of ignorance and superstition, this indulgence was extended to persons who could read, and the monks acquired large sums of money, in artfully teaching criminals to read, and thus screening them from punishments ; but this opened a road to murder and other heinous crimes, there being no bounds to ecclesiastical indulgence.   This was partially repressed by Edward III. ; and Edward VI. decreed that no person guilty of manslaughter, except a peer of the realm, or a priest in holy orders, should claim the benefit of clergy.

BEZANT.   A curious custom formerly prevailed at Shaftesbury, in connection with the water supply, called the " Bezant."   On the Monday before Holy Thursday, a procession, with the bezant, somewhat like a May-day garland, decorated with ribbon, lace, peacocks' feathers, etc., marched to Enmore, half-a-mile distant, and presented a tribute, consisting of a calf's head, a pair of gloves, a gallon of beer, and two penny loaves of white wheaten bread, to the lord of the manor of Gillingham, from whose estate the water is obtained , after which the procession marched back to the Guildhall, preceded by the bezant, which sometimes was hung with gold and jewels borrowed from the inhabitants, to the value, frequently, of £1,800.   The pageant has now fallen into disuse, having been discontinued for forty-three years.   Bezant being the name of an ancient gold coin, we

23

may presume that the ceremony took its name from such a piece of money being originally rendered to the lord of the manor.

BIRTH BADGES. In the city of Haarlem, on the birth of a child, a peculiar ornament of white lace and cardboard, about 5 in. by 4 in., is hung just outside the street door. The inhabitants have had the privilege from time immemorial of using such badges; and that for the period of six weeks after a birth, while such badge was visible, no tax collector or creditor of any kind was allowed to demand payment.

BISHOP AND HIS CLERKS. The rocks west of Pembrokeshire were so called, from an incident which occurred many years ago. Some merchant ships coming from Spain were wrecked there; and it happened that a man, called Miles Bishop, with two others, named Clarke, were the only persons saved, by their clinging fast to the fragment of a mast. Hence the term, the "Bishop and his Clerks."

BISHOP'S APRON. This is nothing more than the short cassock, and is not peculiarly a part of the episcopal dress, for the practice of the bishops wearing it only demonstrates that they are attentive to the spirit of the seventy-fourth canon, which extends its obligation and forces its authority alike on the dignitary and the priest. The short cassock differs from the long one in its having no collar or sleeves, and in its extending only about two inches below the knees. It was so commonly used about a century ago, that there were then various kinds made; some adapted for riding, and others for walking.

24

BISHOPRICS. In England there are two archbishop-rics—Canterbury and York, and twenty-six bishoprics, namely, London, Durham, Winchester, Bath and Wells, Rochester, Peterborough, Lincoln, St. Asaph, Bangor, Worcester, St David's, Carlisle, Llandaff, Chester, Oxford, Gloucester and Bristol, Ely, Exeter, Lichfield and Coventry, Chichester, Ripon, Salisbury, Norwich, Hereford, and Manchester. In Ireland there are two archbishoprics, Dublin and Armagh; and ten bishoprics. There is also the bishopric of the Isle of Sodor and Man, but the bishop does not sit in the House of Lords.

BLOODHOUND. Anciently termed "sleuthound," was of great use and in high esteem among our ancestors. This dog was remarkable for the acuteness of his smell, tracing any wounded game that had escaped from the hunter, and following the footsteps of the thief, let the distance of his flight be ever so great. The bloodhound was in great request on the confines of England and Scotland, when the Borderers were continually preying on the herds and flocks of their neighbours, and was used also by Wallace and Bruce during the civil wars.

BLOWING THE HORN. At Ripon, in Yorkshire, it was formerly the practice to blow a horn at the market cross and the mayor's door, at nine o'clock in the evening; after which, if any house was robbed, the town was taxed to reimburse the sufferer. The horn is still blown, but the tax has been discontinued.

BOATSWAIN'S WHISTLE. This must have been used as early as the time of Shakespeare, who puts the

25

following words in the mouth of the chorus, at the commencement of the third Act of King Henry V. :—

> " Upon the hempen tackle ship-boys climbing,
> Hear the shrill whistle, which doth order give
> To sounds confused."

Again, in the scene of "The Tempest," the boatswain
says, "Tend to the master's whistle."

BODMIN RIDING. A curious custom, called "the
Bodmin Riding," existed at Bodmin, in Cornwall, the inhabitants going in procession on foot and horseback, with
garlands of flowers, to Heilgrave Moor, but of late years it
has fallen into disuse.

BONFIRES. Some people are inclined to suppose that
the name originated with the burning of bones, but it
appears to be an absurd idea; in fact, the historian Stowe
asserts that they took their origin from the reconciliation of
two parties who had been at variance, or had been made
loving friends from the bitterest enemies, when the event
was celebrated by the kindling of a fire of combustibles, etc.
Bon, in French, signifies good, and we have reason to
believe that bonfires were used in crowded cities to purify
the air, and cleanse it from infection.

BONNETS IN CHURCHES. It has been an Eastern
custom, from time immemorial, for females to wear veils
closely attached to their faces, it being considered very
immodest for them to exhibit their features. This custom
is observed to the present day   St. Paul alluded to it in his
epistles (see 1 Cor xi), and condemned the women at
Corinth for being in the house of God with their heads
uncovered · he also directed attention to the preservation

20

of their hair, as being one of their greatest ornaments ; and we find that in all ages, and almost every country, the females endeavour to promote its growth, and set it off to the greatest advantage. Men, on the contrary, except the Quakers, consider the uncovering the head a mark of solemn reverence and respect. (See *Head.*)

BOOKS. The first five books in the Bible, generally called the Pentateuch, ostensibly written by Moses, are considered the oldest books. But on secular subjects, Homer's poems are thought to be so. Before paper was invented, people used various materials in the place of books, such as plates of lead, copper, bark of trees, bricks, stone, wood, etc. The Jewish historian, Josephus, speaks of two columns,—one of stone, the other of brick—on which the children of Seth wrote their inventions and astronomical discoveries. The ten commandments were written on stone, and Solon's laws on wooden planks. The ancients used tablets of wood, box, and ivory, which they sometimes covered with wax, being a material easy to write on, and rub out. (See *Ancient Reading*)

BOOM. This word means a pole, from the German *baum*=a tree, also *segel-baum*=a mast. It is used also for a strong iron chain fastened to a number of spars or strong poles, and stretched across the mouth of a harbour to prevent the entry of the enemy's ships. As a general rule, there is some mechanical contrivance attached to the ends of the boom, so that it may be raised or lowered above or below the surface of the water at the will of the defenders.

BOWING THE BODY. This custom has been observed from time immemorial, particularly in Eastern

-7

countries, where it was common for a man to bow himself before the sovereign till his face touched the ground. The Mohamedans, instead of kneeling whilst at prayers, bow the body very low, with the hands crossed over the breast, or resting on the knee, which is considered still more humble; but the more common bow is a slight inclination of the body, with the right hand laid on the heart, which is thought a sufficient mark of respect towards those in high life.

BOWS AND ARROWS. It is very evident that they were of very ancient use, as we read of them in the book of Genesis. But the bow was brought into this country by the Anglo-Saxons and Danes. The cross-bow was introduced by the Normans. (See *Archery.*)

BOUNDS (Beating the). The custom of perambulating the boundaries of parishes on Ascension-day is a festival well known in modern times, and had its origin in heathenism, in imitation of the feast called "Terminalia," which took place in February, in honour of the god Terminus, who was supposed to preside over bounds and limits, and to punish all unlawful usurpation of land, etc. On this festival the country people assembled together, and crowned the stones which separated their possessions with garlands and flowers, and sprinkled them, in a solemn manner, with the blood of a victim, generally that of a lamb or a young pig, which was offered to the god who presided over the boundaries; libations of wine and milk were also made at the same time.

BRACELETS. In the most ancient period of history the bra.. let .. in ensign of loyalty. In later times, it has been used in the East as a badge of power. The bracelet of Rebekah, mentioned in Genesis, weighed ten shekels, or about five ounces. Among the Romans, the men, as well as the women, wore them, but the latter never wore them till they were betrothed. They were at first properly military ornaments, or rewards, frequently conferred by generals and princes on those who behaved gallantly in fight. The northern people used to swear on their bracelets to render contracts more inviolable. Bracelets made of metal, glass, beads, and the like, are still worn.

BRAY (Vicar of). Bray is a village well known in Berkshire, the vivacious vicar whereof, Pendleton, lived under Henry VIII., Edward VI., Mary, and Elizabeth. He was first a Papist, then a Protestant, then a Papist, and then a Protestant again. This vicar being taxed for being a turn-coat, " Not so," said he ; "for I always kept my principle, which is this :—to live and die vicar of Bray " It is not generally known that he subsequently became a city rector. In the reign of Edward VI., Lawrence Sanders, the martyr, an honest but mild and timorous man, stated to Pendleton his fears that he had not strength of mind to endure the persecution of the times, and was answered by Pendleton, that "he would see every drop of his fat and the last morsel of his flesh consumed to ashes ere he would swerve from the faith then established." He, however, changed with the times, saved his fat and his flesh, and became rector of St. Stephen's, Walbrook, while Sanders was burnt in Smithfield.

BRAZENNOSE COLLEGE. This strange name originated in the circumstance of its having been erected on the site of two ancient halls, one of which was called Brazennose

29

Hall, on account of an iron ring fixed in a nose of brass, which served as a knocker to the gate.

BRIDECAKE. This term originated in the Roman custom called *confarreation*, or dividing a cake made of wheat or barley (from the Latin *far*, bread or corn), as an emblem of firm alliance between man and wife. The custom of breaking a cake over the wife's head when she entered her husband's house was derived from the Greeks, who poured fruit and figs over the heads of the bride and bridegroom, as an emblem of future plenty. Dr. Moffat tells us that the " English, when the bride came from the church, were wont to sprinkle wheat upon her head."

BRITONS. Some writers assert that the word Britons, as applied to the ancient inhabitants of Britain, originated with Brute, a Trojan prince, who settled in the island with his companions after the overthrow of Troy. Others suppose that the word is a corruption of Britain, *bri* implying honour, and *tain* a river,—the island abounding in rivers ; or from the word *bryth*, painted or stained, as the inhabitants used to dye or stain their bodies with a herb of that name.

BULL (John). This expression took its rise from Dean Swift's humorous history of Europe, wherein the English people were thus personified. He also called the sovereign of Austria, Squire South ; the sovereign of Spain, Street ; and that of France, Louis Baboon.

BUMPER It is usual at convivial parties to drink what is termed a bumper—that is, the contents of a glass brim full This had its origin, it is said, with the Catholics, who usually drank the Pope's health every day after dinner in a full glass, with the expression in French—*au bon père* (to the good father). Hence the term bumper.

BUNS (Hot Cross). Eating buns on Good Friday was a sort of reverential custom in commemoration of the death of Christ on the cross. These buns have the sign of the cross imprinted on them, and are now to be met with in almost every town in the kingdom. The uneducated still have a superstition, that if they carefully dry these cakes, and grate them into powder, they are infallible against many diseases.

BURYING-GROUNDS. The custom of burying the dead in enclosed grounds set apart for that purpose, was established about the year 200. Before that time people were interred in caves, under trees, and in the highways. Ancient tombs still exist by roads near Rome, from which the words so often seen in modern epitaphs are derived—namely, " *Siste, viator*," Stop, traveller.

BUTTON LAW. By Act of Parliament passed in three reigns—William III., Anne, and George I.—it was illegal for tailor to make, or man to wear, clothes with any other buttons appended thereto but of brass. This law came in force for the benefit of the Birmingham makers ; and it enacted, not only that he who made or sold garments with any but brass buttons pay a penalty of forty shillings for every dozen, but that he should not be able to recover the debt if the wearer thought proper to resist payment.

BY JINGO. A common oath, said to be a corruption of St. Gingoulph ; it has likewise been taken as a corruption of Jove or Jupiter.

31

C.

CANDLEMAS. So called from the abundance of consecrated candles formerly used on the 2nd of February
(or Purification of the Virgin Mary) by the primitive
Christians in their processions. This custom was prohibited by Edward VI., but is still observed by the Catholics.

CANDLES. The origin of candles is obscure. They
were first used to light cathedrals and churches, and were
made of wax. History records that Alfred the Great employed a graduated wax candle, enclosed in a lantern, as
the best mode then known for marking the divisions of
time. Candles were not in general use for domestic purposes till towards the close of the thirteenth century, when
they are first noticed as being made of tallow.

CARDINAL. An ecclesiastical prince of the Romish
Church, who has a voice in the conclave at the election of a
pope, who is chosen from them. The number of cardinals
is seventy—namely, six bishops, fifty priests, and fourteen
deacons. These constitute the sacred college, and are
chosen by the pope.

CARDS. We may trace the origin of playing cards to
sacred and profane history. The four kings represent
David, Alexander, Cæsar, and Charles, which names are
still retained on the French cards. They also indicate the
four monarchies of the Jews, Greeks, Romans, and Franks,
under Charlemagne. The consorts of these historic personages were Arginè, Esther, Judith, and Pallas, typical of
birth, piety, fortitude, and wisdom. Arginè is merely a
transposition of letter, and implies the queen by

32

descent. By the knaves we understand the servants or valets of the kings, as knave originally meant a servant, or armour-bearer. We have no account of playing cards having been used till the reign of Charles V. of France. The word ace is derived from the Greek *eis*, signifying one, *as*, French. *Trèfle* is the French word for "clubs," and implies clover, which is easily distinguished by its being painted similar to that plant. *Pique*, the French for "spades," means pike, intimating that a magazine of arms should be well supplied. Diamond, in French, implies *carreau*, by which is meant a square, also a particular kind of arrow, but in a military sense it means that the soldiers should have their arms complete before going to battle. *Cœur*, the French for "heart," denotes courage or bravery of the soldiers.

CAROLS. These have had a remarkable history. At one time they were church hymns, and that only ; at another, although still hymns of religious joy, they were intended rather for domestic than church use ; while in another phase, they were elements in Christmas festivity, neither evincing religious thoughts nor couched in reverent language. As to the word itself, etymologists are not agreed whether it was derived directly from the Latin, or mediately through the French or Italian ; but the meaning has always been accepted as that of a hymn of joy, especially as applied to those intended for Christmas. It has been said, that the first carol was the song of the angels mentioned by St. Luke, "Glory to God in the highest," for it was a song of joy in relation to the nativity. It is known that the bishops and clergy, after the apostolic times, were wont to sing carols together in church on Christmas-day. (See *Hymns*.)

D

CASH. This word is derived from the Italian *cassa,* the chest in which Italian merchants kept their money, as do at the present time the Spaniards in their *caja,* the Portuguese in their *caxa,* and the French in their *caisse.* The application of the word cash to money is altogether English, it not having any corresponding term in any other European language. *Cash* having been so inconsiderately adopted instead of *cassa* (chest), entries in the cash-book (it should be chest-book) are made in the English counting.houses in this unmeaning way, " Cash Dr." and " Cash Cr."—whereas the chest, and not the money, is Dr. for what is taken out.

CATHERINE WHEEL. Tradition mentions that St. Catherine lived at Alexandria, where she preached the gospel, and converted numbers to Christianity, among whom were fifty philosophers. This excited the jealousy of the emperor Maxentius, who cast her into prison, and ordered one of his artificers to invent an engine of extraordinary torture. This was constructed with four wheels, with saws, knives, and sharp nails, which ran against each other. The saint being bound to one of these wheels, and the other turned the contrary way, an angel struck the wheel, which flew to pieces, and killed a great number of her persecutors, whilst she remained unhurt. Those who survived cried " Great is the God of the Christians," and were all converted, which so incensed the emperor that he ordered her to be beheaded.

CAT'S WHISKERS. The use of these in a state of nature is very important. They are attached to a bed of glands under the skin, and each of these long hairs is connected with the nerves of the lip ; the slightest contact of these whiskers with any surrounding object is thus felt

34

most distinctly by the animal, although the hairs themselves are insensible. Whiskers are a common appendage to the feline family. They stand out on each side of the lion as well as the common cat ; so that from point to point, they are equal to the width of the animal's body.

CATS (why they see in the dark). The pupil of the eye of the cat is of an oval form, the transverse diameter being parallel to the nose, and cats have the power of contracting or dilating the pupil at pleasure. We observe that it is always contracted either in the sun or before a fire ; this prevents a painful sensation which would be occasioned by a number of rays of light falling on the pupil; but when a cat sits in the shade, or in the dark, she fully dilates the pupil, which enables her to see and seize her prey.

CHAMPION. The office of Champion of England was first instituted in the reign of Richard II. On the sovereign's coronation day, he rides up Westminster Hall, on a white horse, proclaiming the monarch by the usual titles ; then throws down a gauntlet, or iron glove, challenging any one to take it up and fight him, who does not believe the monarch then present to be lawful heir to the crown.

CHARING-CROSS. Eleanor of Castile, a most beautiful woman, and wife to Edward I., died in Nottinghamshire, and was buried in Westminster Abbey When her remains were being carried thither, Edward caused a stone cross to be erected wherever the body rested ; the last was at Charing, hence the word Charing-Cross.

CHARTER-PARTY. A charter-party is a covenant entered into between merchants and masters of ships relating to the ship and cargo. It is said to have been first used in England about 1243.

CHEQUERS. Some people imagine that the chequers painted on the door-posts of public-houses are meant to show that the game of draughts might be played there, but this is erroneous; the chequers were first used in the time of William the Conqueror, who was related to the Earl of Warrenne and Surrey. This nobleman, whose family arms were the chequers, espoused the cause of William, who accorded to him the exclusive right of granting licences for the sale of malt liquor; and in order to enable the agents to collect the consideration money more readily, the door-posts were painted with those arms. This privilege was exercised so recently as the reign of William and Mary.

CHERUBIM. The words Cherubim and Seraphim, used in that part of the church service commonly called " Te Deum," are derived from the Hebrew, and imply knowledge and flame. It was generally supposed by the ancients, that cherubim mean those angels who possess a superior knowledge of the Almighty, and that seraphim, or flame, are those who excel in their love to Him.

CHICKENS (Mother Cary's). Mariners consider that the sight of a petrel predicts a storm, and the reason for its appearance is thus given—" Because petrels seem to repose in a common breeze; but upon the approach or during the continuation of a gale, they surround a ship, and catch up the small animals which the agitated ocean brings near the surface, or any food that may be dropped from the vessel. Whisking like an arrow through the deep valleys of the abyss, and darting away over the foaming crest of some

3

mountain wave, they attend the labouring barque in all her perilous course. When the storm subsides they retire to rest, and are no more seen. Our sailors have from very early times called these birds 'Mother Cary's chickens.'" (See *Stormy Petrel.*)

CHILDREN (of Fox Island). The treatment of these children is very singular. The parents feed them when very young with the coarsest flesh, and generally raw. If an infant cries, the mother immediately carries it to the seaside, and plunges it in the water till it is quiet. This is done in the coldest day of winter, and instead of hurting the children, it hardens and inures them to the severity of the climate, and enables them to go barefoot throughout the winter.

CHILTERN HUNDREDS. These are certain lands in Buckinghamshire, Hertford, and Oxford, belonging to the crown, and when a member of parliament wishes to vacate his seat, he accepts the stewardship of these lands, at a salary of twenty shillings per annum. As the English law will allow no M.P. to hold office under the crown unless he be re-elected, the acceptance of this is made a kind of subterfuge for his resignation.

CHIVALRY. In the year 1369 John II., Duke de Bourbon, instituted an order of chivalry. One of the statutes of it is curious, and shows the high opinion he entertained of the influence of the female sex upon the virtue and happiness of mankind. According to this statute, the knights were obliged to pay due respect to all ladies, both married and unmarried, and never to suffer anything derogatory to their reputation to be said in their presence;

37

" for," adds the statute, " those who speak ill of women have very little honour, and (to their disgrace be it mentioned) say of that sex which cannot revenge itself what they would not dare to say of a man ; for from women, after God, arises a great part of the honour that there is in the world."

CHRISTMAS BOXES. It was anciently a custom to carry a box from door to door, for the collection of little presents at Christmas. In an old work entitled " The Athenian Oracle," it is stated that, formerly, it was a custom for the monks to offer masses for the safety of all ships that went on long voyages, to each of which a little box was affixed (under the custody of the priest), into which the sailors put money or other valuables, in order to secure the prayers of the church. At Christmas these boxes were opened, and were thence called " Christmas boxes." In order that no person, however indigent, should omit these presents, the poor were encouraged to beg " box-money " of their richer neighbours, to enable them to add to the priest's perquisites. The custom of " boxing " has been observed throughout England to the present day.

CHRISTMAS-DAY. This is so named from the *Christi Missa,* the Mass of Christ, and thence the Roman Catholic Liturgy is termed Mass Book. About the year 500, the observance of this day became general in the Catholic Church.

CHURCH NOSEGAYS. The following curious custom exists on the Elbe :—The peasantry who possess a bit of land, however small, never enter the church without having a nosegay in the hands. They thus intend, it is said, to show that they claim the consideration due to persons who

38

possess some property in the parish.   Among the country people in the neighbourhood of Hamburg, there is no garden so small as not to possess a place for the flowers intended for this use, and the plat is distinguished by the name of "the church nosegay."

CHURCH (The First).   The first church in England was erected at Glastonbury, in Somersetshire, in the early part of the second century.   It was made of wicker-work. The first made of stone was at St. Piran, Cornwall.

CHURCHES ON HILLS.   Building churches on high hills probably had its origin among the Greeks, who worshipped their gods on the top of high mountains   The nations who resided near Judæa sacrificed upon mountains, or heaven-kissing hills.   Balak carried Balaam to the top of different mountains to sacrifice.   Abraham offered up his son Isaac on a mountain in Moriah.   In later ages temples were built on high mountains.   Lofty hills were sacred to the gods, because their tops approached nearer to heaven, the supposed seat of the heathen deities : and as the primitive Christians observed the rites and customs of the heathens to a certain extent, it is very probable that they built their churches on the most elevated spots they could find.

CHURCHES (Why decorated).   This custom had its origin in paganism ; the heathens having been in the habit of adorning the temples, altars, and images of their favourite deity, whose festival they celebrated, with such shrubs and boughs of trees as they considered were agreeable to him. The ivy, in particular, was devoted to Bacchus, emblematic of his being always young   The Greeks named Bacchus "*Bromius,*" which the Romans translated Bruma, and his

39

feasts were celebrated at the winter solstice, or Bruma ; the primitive Christians were much inclined to observe heathen festivals, fearing that if they abandoned them at once, it might prove injurious to that religion which they had adopted. Hence the custom of decorating churches and houses with shrubs and branches at Christmas and other festivals.

CHURCHING OF WOMEN. This, like many other Christian ceremonies, took its rise from the Jewish rite of purification, ordered by the law of Moses. In the Eastern Churches the period was limited to forty days after a birth, but in western Europe no time is observed. Being a portion of our Liturgy, it is observed as a mode of thanksgiving, and practised in England, generally within a month after child-birth.

CINDERELLA. The following story, which Burton, in his " Anatomy of Melancholy," quotes, is obviously the origin of one of our most popular nursery tales :—" Rhodope was the fairest ladie in her dayes in all Egypt; she went to wash her, and by chance (her maidens meanwhile looking but carelessly to her clothes), an eagle stole away one of her shoes, and laid it in Psammeticus, the king of Egypt's lap, at Memphis. He wondered at the excellency of the shoe and pretty foot, but more at the manner of the bringing of it, and caused forthwith proclamation to be made that she that owned that shoe should come presently to his court ; the virgin came, and was forthwith married to the king."

CINQUE PORTS. The word *cinque* is derived from the French, meaning five. They were originally instituted

40

and incorporated by William the Conqueror, who granted them many privileges, conditionally, that they would, in time of war, furnish him with ships well manned and armed, free of expense. They were Dover, Hastings, Romney, Hythe, and Sandwich; but subsequently Rye, Seaford, and Winchelsea were included with the former.

CITY SWORDS. There are four swords belonging to the citizens of London. 1. The Sword of State, borne before the Lord Mayor, as the emblem of his civic authority. This is the sword which is surrendered to the sovereign at Temple Bar, when she comes within the city of London. 2. Another is called the Pearl Sword, from the nature of its ornaments, and is carried before the Lord Mayor on all occasions of ceremony or festivity. 3. The third is a sword placed at the Central Criminal Court above the Lord Mayor's chair. 4. The fourth is a Black Sword, to be used in Lent, on days of public fasts, and on the death of any of the Royal Family.

CLARION. The clarion was invented by the Moors in Spain, about the year 800. It was at first a trumpet, serving as a treble to others sounding tenor and bass.

CLIPPER. This is an Anglo-Saxon term for "one who runs fast." It is now applied to ships which are noted for their speed. Clippers are much sharper in the bows than other vessels.

CLOCKS. Various machines were doubtless employed at a very remote date, for the purpose of measuring time, but the most ancient clock made upon principles similar to the clocks of the present day, was constructed by Henry de Wyck, a German artist, in 1364, and placed by him in the

41

tower of the palace of Charles V., of France. It struck the hours, but did not record so small a portion of time as minutes. Clockmakers were first introduced into England in 1368, when Edward III. granted a licence to three of these artists to come over from Delft, in Holland, and practise their occupation in this country. The earliest portable clock of which any account has been given, is one dated 1525, made by Jacob Lech, of Prague. The oldest English clock extant is said to be one in a turret of Hampton Court Palace, constructed in the year 1540, by a maker whose initials are N. O.

CLUB LAW. In the canton of Valais, a singular custom was formerly practised when it was intended to drive away any powerful and obnoxious member of the state. A large club was provided, the end of which was rudely carved into the shape of a man's head, the supposed representation of the obnoxious party. Every one who wished his expulsion drove a nail in this club, and when the number of nails was thought to be sufficiently great, this emblem was carried in procession before the house of the offender, who was summoned to justify his conduct; but he was already condemned without being heard in his defence, and ordered to emigrate in a certain time. If he refused to obey the sentence, his house was attacked and pillaged.

COCKER (According to) The popular use of the phrase, "according to Cocker," when anything is done quite right, and admits of no question or improvement, refers to Cocker, who was born about the year 1632, and died between 1671 and 1677. He was the author of a work on arithmetic, which obtained great popularity, and ran through a large number of editions. Almost all the

42

systems of arithmetic that have since been published in Great Britain, for the use of schools, have followed his method very closely ; and, as many of them professed on the title-page to be "according to Cocker," the expression gained general currency. The Americans do not use this expression, but "according to Gunter," a distinguished English mathematician, who was born in 1581, and died in 1626. He is best known as the inventor of the chain commonly used by surveyors for measuring land, and of the flat wooden rule marked with scales of equal parts, of sines, chords, etc., and also with logarithms, of these various parts—which is used to solve problems in surveying and navigation, mechanically, with the aid of the dividers alone.

COCKNEY. In the reign of Edward III , a knight held some land at Cukeney, in Nottinghamshire, free of rent, during the reign of the king, on condition of his shoeing the king's palfrey, or saddle-horse, on each foot with the kings nails and materials ; but, if he lamed it, he was to give the king another worth four marks. The knight of Cukeney attended at the king's stable to perform his duty, when one of the monarch's farriers offered to instruct him how to do it ; but in order to save his purse, he declined the offer, and consequently, by his ignorance, lamed the horse. This he continued to do till he had to forfeit more marks than the value of the land, by which act of folly the word became proverbial, even at court, and every stupid, untutored citizen, was called a Cukeney Knight, which was afterwards changed to Cockney, a nickname still borne by Londoners. Many derivations are given of this word Halliwell states, in his essay upon this word, that "some writers trace the word with much pro-

43

babily to the imaginary land of Cockaygne, the lubber land of the olden time." Others, that a person born in London, could not distinguish between a cock's crow and horse's neigh, being so ignorant of country sounds.

COMMONS (House of). The commons are not the Parliament, neither are the Lords, nor the Crown ; but the three united are the " Estates," which in their triple capacity, constitute the Parliament, and exercise the legislative functions of the realm. (See *Parliament.*) A peer is, therefore, as much a member of parliament as a commoner ; while the Crown is an entire state of parliament, centered in the person of an individual. The two Houses, convened by royal authority, and acting jointly with the Crown, constitute the Legislature, or Parliament, and its acts are called indifferently, " Statutes," or " Acts of Parliament." They have the full force and effect of law.

CONDITION. This word is applied in law to any contingency, upon the happening of which it is provided in any lease or other document conveying an interest in real property, that such interest shall either be increased or diminished, or shall altogether cease and determine.

CONFIRMATION. This ceremony is said to have descended from the apostles, and to be founded on their example and practice. In the early ages of Christianity, it was observed immediately after baptism, if the bishop happened to be present. This is still continued among the Greeks, and throughout the Eastern Churches. But the Catholics make it a distinct sacrament, after a person has attained the age of seven years. In England, however, no

44

particular time is insisted on ; but the clergy are scrupulous of admitting persons to this ceremony under fourteen.

CONSTABLE OF ENGLAND. The office of Constable of England (*Comes Stabuli*, Great Master of the Horse, such being then the principal military force), was an office of the highest dignity in early times ; the holder during war being next in rank to the king. He was the king's lieutenant, and commanded in his absence. He inspected and certified the military contingents furnished by the barons and knights, etc, such being the only national force in those days. He was in close attendance on the king in time of peace also ; he and the king's "justiciar" alone witnessing the king's writs, and he had the power of arresting the sheriffs of counties for the neglect of their duties, etc. The last High Constable of England was Stafford, Duke of Buckingham, beheaded in the reign of Henry VIII., who abolished the office through jealousy of its high privileges. The *bâton* of the duke has, however, been carefully preserved by his descendants, and is now in possession of Lord Stafford. Baker in his " Chronicle," says, " that it was the greatest place, next the high steward, in the kingdom ; and that the power of the High Constable tended to restrain some actions of the king. No wonder that the jealous tyrant (Henry VIII.) declared that the office was too great for a subject, and that in future he would hold it himself."

CONSTELLATIONS. On the celestial globe the stars are divided into different groups, which are called constellations, under the form or outline of some assumed animal or figure, such as the ancient astronomers supposed these groups to represent. They are still retained, for the

45

sake of distinction, and to direct the astronomer. The word itself means an assemblage or system of several stars, and was introduced by the ancient Chaldæans, Babylonians, or Assyrians, who were famous for their skill in astronomy; and it is imagined that they were the first people who reduced it to a science, from whom it was handed down to the Egyptians, from the Egyptians to the Greeks, from the Greeks to the Romans, and from the Romans to ourselves.

COPYRIGHT Paying five shillings and filling up a printed form at Stationers' Hall, formerly secured the copyright of an English book for forty-two years, or for seven years after the death of the author. But by 5 & 6 Vic. c. 45, copyright is now extended to the author's life, and seven years after his death; or if this shall fall short of forty-two years, then for forty-two years from the first publication. Four copies of the complete work must also be sent to Stationers' Hall, and one copy to the British Museum. Copyright is personal property, and may be transferred, leased, or rented.

COQUETTE. This word is thus defined by Cotgrave in 1611, namely.—"A prattling or proud gossip; a fisking or fliperous minx; a cocket, or tattling housewife; a titifill, flibergebit." The meaning of cocket may be judged from its synonyms in another place: "Indiscreetly peart, jollie, cheerful; more bold than welcome, forwarder than wise."

CORK. This material is the exterior bark of a tree of the oak species, which grows wild in the southern parts of Europe, particularly France, Spain, Portugal, and Italy. When the tree is about twenty six years old, it is fit to be barked, and this can be done successively every eight years. The bark always grows again, and its quality improves with the increasing age of the tree. It is singular, however, that glass bottles, which were introduced in the fifteenth century, had no cork stoppers till near the end of the seventeenth century, when they were first used in the apothecaries' shops in Germany. Wine and oil flasks are, even now, stopped merely with oiled cotton in some parts of Italy, as adopted by the ancient Greeks and Romans.

CORPSE CANDLES. These are indigenous to Cambria, and there are many fictitious tales respecting them, for doubtless were a Will-o'-the-wisp seen it would be instantly set down for a corpse candle. It appears that these lights are always observed to veer their course toward the churchyard, which they enter, and after hovering over the spot where the destined victim of death is to be buried, disappear, the light varies in brilliancy and size according to the person whose doom it is to leave the world. The colour is said to be a sulphurous blue, and sometimes red. The reason of their appearing in Wales, report says, is because a bishop of St. David's in days of yore, prayed that they might be seen before a person's death, in order to impress the minds of people that they might be fitted to depart to another world.

CORPUS CHRISTI. This festival, " the body of Christ," was appointed in honour of the Eucharist, and always falls on the Thursday after Trinity Sunday. In Catholic countries, this is the only day in the year when the *consecrated Host* is exposed in the streets of the different cities and towns to the gaze of the adoring multitude. It is called the *fête Dieu,* and is one of the most remarkable

47

festivals of the Romish Church, beginning on Trinity Sunday, and ending on the Sunday following.

COTTON.   The cotton plant was anciently to be found only in Egypt.   Certainly, the raw material was introduced into Europe long before the discovery of the passage to India by the Cape of Good Hope; and it appears that this country was supplied with it, from the Levant, by the Genoese vessels in 1430.   The first certain information respecting the cotton manufactures of England is contained in Lewis Roberts' "Treasures of Traffic," published in 1641, in which he states that "the people of Manchester buy cotton wool that comes from Cyprus and Smyrna, and work the same into fustians, vermilions, and dimities, which are sent to London and sold or exported." (See *Spinning.*)

COURSING.   As early as about B.C. 400, Xenophon wrote a treatise on coursing   The Gauls, it appears, first introduced this healthful exercise.   Early in the morning the serfs of the nobles went out with the dogs to find the hares; after which the masters went in pursuit of them.   In the reign of Elizabeth, when the ladies of the court, instead of tea and bread-and-butter, took for their breakfast good roast beef, washed down by stout brown ale, and then spent a whole day on horseback, coursing was so popular a recreation that her majesty ordered the Duke of Norfolk to draw up a code of laws for its regulation, which even now is held in great respect by sportsmen.

COURT OF ARRAY.   At Lichfield, on Whit-Monday, what is called the "court of array of men-at-arms" is still held; formerly it was a splendid ceremonial, but now it is merely a procession of the charities of the town, accom-

48

panied by men in armour, and signalised by a gratuitous supply of refreshments to all comers.

COVENANT. Is a mutual consent, or agreement, of two or more persons, to do or to forbear some act or thing. A covenant is created by deed in writing, sealed and executed; or it may be implied in the contract. In Church affairs, a solemn agreement between the members of a Church, that they will walk together according to the precepts of the gospel, in brotherly affection.

CREED (Apostles'). The articles of the Christian faith were originally only the Apostles' Creed. St. Ambrose, Bishop of Milan—the composer of that beautiful portion of our Liturgy entitled "*Te Deum Laudamus*"—alleges it was written by the twelve apostles before they set out on their mission of Christianity, as a key to their common opinion. Other writers assert that each apostle composed one article, in the following order: St Peter gave us the first—I believe in God the Father Almighty. St. John—Maker of heaven and earth. James—And in Jesus Christ His only Son our Lord. Andrew—Who was conceived by the Holy Ghost, born of the Virgin Mary. Philip—Suffered under Pontius Pilate, was crucified, dead, and buried. Thomas—He descended into hell; the third day He rose again from the dead. Bartholomew—He ascended into heaven, and sitteth on the right hand of God the Father Almighty. Matthew—From thence He shall come to judge the quick and the dead. James, son of Alpheus—I believe in the Holy Ghost, the Holy Catholic Church. Simon—The communion of Saints; the forgiveness of sins. Jude, brother of James—The resurrection of the body. Matthias—And the life everlasting. Amen.

CRIMINALS (Stupefying). Intoxicating draughts used anciently to be given to malefactors just before their execution, to stupefy, and render them insensible to pain. The compassionate ladies of Jerusalem generally provided this potion, which consisted of frankincense and wine, at their own cost. This humane custom was first adopted by king Solomon.

CROOKED SIXPENCE. A bent coin is often given in the west of England, for luck, as it is termed, and a crooked sixpence is usually selected by careful grandmothers, aunts, and uncles, to bestow as the "hanselling" of a new purse.

CROSSES (Stone). These are very often placed at cross roads, and are to be met with in different parts of England. They are still more numerous on the Continent, and are of great antiquity, as we read in the book of Genesis that Jacob erected a stone pillar, which custom possibly has been handed down to successive generations.

CROWN AND SCEPTRE. The sceptre is of much greater antiquity than the crown. The poet Homer, 884 B.C , speaks of the sceptre, and the elder Tarquin assumed it 577 B.C. We also read of the sceptre in the book of Esther. It appears that crowns were first worn as a religious decoration, and not to constitute a monarch. The crown was first used as a kingly ornament by the Emperor Aurelian, about 275 B.C. The first imperial, or double crown, was worn by Edward IV.

CROWN OFFICERS. The principal public functionaries in the order of precedence are—the Lord Chancellor, First Lord of the Treasury (Prime Minister). Lord President of the Privy Council, Lord Privy Seal, Chancellor of the Exchequer, · Secretary of State for the Home Department, Secretary of State for Foreign Affairs, Colonial Secretary, Secretary of State for the War Department, Secretary of State for the Government of India, First Lord of the Admiralty, President of the Board of Trade, Chief Commissioner of Works, President of the Poor Law Board, the Post Master General, and many others.

CRUCIFIXION. The ancient Jews and other Eastern nations considered the death of the cross the most dreadful that could be inflicted, both for disgrace and torture, and it was so execrable that it was inflicted only as a mark of detestation on the vilest people. Moses himself commanded that a person executed in this way should not remain on the cross after sunset, he being utterly despised by many and accursed by God. The cross itself has, however, been a subject of adoration in the ancient Church, and is still worshipped by Roman Catholics.

CURATE. A curate signifies an assistant to the incumbent, vicar, or rector of a church, who performs Divine service in his stead, for which he receives a salary. A layman means any person not in holy orders, one of the laity or people, in distinction from the clergy.

CURFEW BELL. This means cover-fire bell, and was instituted by William the Conqueror, who had it rung in every town at eight o'clock in the evening, to warn all his subjects to put out their fires and candles, under the penalty of a heavy fine. Although still rung in many places at eight o'clock, the penalty was abolished in 1100.

CZAR. The title of Czar is a corruption of Cæsar It

was first used as a title by Ivan II. of Russia, about the year
1579. The Russian word is, however, written *Tsar.*

D.

DAGGER MONEY. Newcastle-upon-Tyne is one of
the towns in the kingdom which lodge and maintain Her
Majesty's commission of assize, and attendants, during the
assizes for the county of Northumberland, as a matter of
obligation from prescriptive usage The mayor at each
assize presents the judge with £1 10s., the value of a gold
coin of James II , as a conduct or " dagger money " to the
next assize town—a relic of the days when the Border Moss-
troopers rendered the presence of a mounted guard indispensable to safe-conduct.

DANCING. Among the priests of Egypt, dancing was
held in great respect, and formed no inconsiderable portion
of their sacred rites. The Hebrews also attached great
importance to the practice : we find them dancing around
the golden calf reared by Aaron in the desert. We further
read that the daughters of Shiloh danced in a yearly feast of
the Lord ; and David danced, to signify his joy that the ark
of God had again been brought into Sion. To complete
the obsequies of the great, to celebrate triumphs in war,
and to mark gratitude to the Giver of all good for any
signal interposition of His mercy, dancing was considered
necessary. Scaliger says, the first bishops were called in
Latin *præsules*, for no other reason but that they led the
solemn dance in great festivals; and the antiquarian, Claude
Menestrier, writing at the latter end of the 17th century,
says, that he had seen the canons and choristers on Whit-
Sunday take each other by the hand and dance, while they

sang hymns of jubilation. The very word "choir" is, he adds, derived from a Greek word, which means *dance.* It is a well-known fact, the descendants of the original inhabitants of our island, the Cambro-Britons, were usually played out of the church by a fiddle, to form a dance in the churchyard at the conclusion of the sermon ; and among our legal usages, till within a century and a half of this time, it may be mentioned that one dance was reserved to be annually performed by the judges of the land. (See *Derry down.*)

DAYS OF THE WEEK. The names of these are derived from Saxon idolatry. The Saxons had seven deities more particularly adored than the rest ; namely, the Sun, Moon, Tuisco, Woden, Thor, Friga, and Seater. *Sunday* being dedicated to the Sun, was called by them Sunandaeg ; his idol represented the bust of a man, with the face darting bright rays, holding a wheel before his breast, indicative of the circuit of the golden orb around our sphere. *Monday* was dedicated to the Moon, and was represented by a female on a pedestal, with a very singular dress, and two long ears. *Tuesday* was consecrated to Tuisco, a German hero, sire of the Germans, Scythians, and Saxons ; he was represented as a venerable old man, with a long white beard, a sceptre in his hand, and the skin of a wild boar thrown over his shoulders. *Wednesday* was consecrated to Woden, or Odin, a supreme god of the northern nations, father of the gods, god of war, or Mars ; he was represented as a warrior in a bold martial attitude, clad in armour, holding in his right hand a broad crooked sword, and a shield in his left. *Thursday* was consecrated to Thor, eldest son of Woden, who was the Roman Jupiter; he was believed to govern the air, preside over lightning and thunder, direct the winds, rain, and seasons ;

53

he was represented as sitting on a splendid throne, with a crown of gold, adorned with twelve glittering stars, and a sceptre in his right hand. *Friday* or Friga, Hertha or Edith, was the mother of the gods, and wife of Woden, she was the goddess of love and pleasure, and was portrayed as a female, with a naked sword in her right hand and a bow in her left, implying that in extreme cases women should fight as well as men. *Saturday*, or Seater, is the same as the Roman Saturnus ; he was represented on a pedestal, standing on the back of a prickly fish called a perch, his head bare, with a thin meagre face ; in his left hand he held a wheel, and in his right a pail of water, with fruits and flowers. The sharp fins of a fish implied that the worshippers of Seater should pass safely through every difficulty. The wheel was emblematic of their unity and freedom, and the pail of water implied that he would water the earth and make it fruitful.

DEACON. The office of deacon was instituted by the apostles. Seven persons were chosen at first, to serve at the feasts of Christians, and distribute bread and wine to the communicants, and to minister to the wants of the poor. In the Church of England, the deacons assist the clergy in administering the holy communion; their office in Presbyterian Churches is to attend to the secular interests, and in Independent Churches it is the same, and also to distribute the bread and wine to the communicants.

DEAD AS A DOOR NAIL. This proverbial expression is more often used than understood. The *door nail* is the *nail* on which, in ancient doors, the knocker strikes. It is, therefore, used as a comparison to any one irrecoverably dead—one who has fallen (as Virgil says) *multâ morte, i.e.*

with abundant death, such as a reiteration of strokes on the head would naturally produce.   Shakespeare wrote ·—

> *Falstaff*—What ! is the old king dead ⁹
> *Pistol*—As *nail in door*.   The things I speak are just.

DEAN   A dean is a prime dignitary in a cathedral or collegiate church, being usually the president of the chapter. Chapter, in canon law, means a congregation of clergymen under the authority of a president or dean.

DEATH WATCH.   This is a small insect about the size of a wood-louse, which makes a ticking noise, like a watch, in the walls of houses and the frames of pictures, particularly in summer   The noise is the call of the male insect to the female, and is often the cause of great alarm to ignorant people, who consider it as a token of the death of a friend.

DEED.   A document which is not only signed but sealed and delivered by the parties thereto   At the present day the seals generally consist of wafers affixed at the end of the signatures, and the delivery is usually made by each party placing his finger on the wafer, which represents his seal, and saying " I deliver this as my act and deed." (See *Seals.*)

DEGREES (Granting of).   Irnerius, the celebrated jurist, is said to have introduced the degree of Doctor into the universities.   The first ceremony of this kind was performed at Bologna, on the person of Bulgarus, in the year 1130, who began to profess the Roman law, and on that occasion was promoted to the doctorate.   The custom was soon transferred from the faculty of the law to that of theology; and Peter Lombard is the first doctor in sacred

55

theology upon record in the university of Paris. Ancient English writers hold the venerable Bede to have been the first doctor of Cambridge, and John de Beverley at Oxford; the latter died in 712. But Spelman thinks there was no title or degree in England till about the year 1207. John Hambois is supposed to be the first musician who was honoured with the title of doctor in England. Holinshed, in his "Chronicles," tells us: "John Hambois was an excellent musician, and for his notable cunning therein he was made a doctor of music."

DEMISE is a granting or letting of land for any, less than a freehold, interest.

DEODAND Formerly, when a person was killed by a mill, cart, horse, or anything moveable, that which was the cause of his death became forfeited to the reigning sovereign, whose almoner was appointed to bestow the value in charity, and it was therefore called "deodand," from *Deo dandum*, as being to be given away for God's sake. This law was abolished in 1846.

DERBY AND OAKS. The Epsom meeting is of some antiquity, having been founded by James I. during his residence at Nonsuch The fact of Epsom being the first mineral spring of fashionable resort in this country, together with its convenient distance from London, materially contributed to its success as a racing town. The Derby, of all races the most popular, was not established till 1780; the first Oaks having been run for the previous year. As may be surmised, it was the Earl of Derby who gave the title to the former race, while that of the latter was named from " The Oaks." his seat in the locality

DERRY DOWN The general burthen to almost all our old English ballads is well known to be "Derry down, derry down, hey derry down:" these words formerly constituted the chorus to the Druidical hymns; the literal signification is, "Let us dance round the oak;" and we may therefore reasonably conclude that dancing formed a necessary part of the religion of the ancient Britons.

DEUS EX MACHINA. This expression is commonly applied to persons who, not being able to escape from a difficulty by ordinary means, have recourse to very unusual ones. It originated in the custom of the tragic poets of ancient Greece, who were in the habit of bringing about their catastrophe by the intervention of some deity, who descended upon the stage out of a car let down by machinery, when the situation of the drama had become too complicated for mere mortals to unravel. Thus the term "*A god out of a machine*" came to be employed on every occasion, and so frequently as to call for the condemnation of Horace, who gives this maxim :—"*Nec deus intersit, nisi dignus vindice nodus*" (Let not a deity interpose, unless the circumstances be worthy of his interference).

DIADEM. This was originally a kind of ribbon tied round the head. Pliny says that Bacchus, the god of wine, was the inventor of it, and Athæneus asserts that topers and drunkards made use of them to preserve themselves from the ill effects of the fumes of wine, by tying them tightly round their foreheads. The pope usually wears a triple crown or diadem, called a tiara.

DIAMONDS (Nine of). The Nine of Diamonds has been called the Curse of Scotland, and various reasons have

57

been assigned ; but that which appears the most credible, is from a Scotch Member of Parliament, whose family arms were the nine of diamonds, having voted for the malt tax in Scotland.

DIEU ET MON DROIT. By this is meant "God and my right," and has been the motto of the royal arms since the defeat of the French by Richard I , at Gisors, in Normandy, in 1198, the French monarch's parole for the day being "*Dieu et mon droit.*" The motto of Queen Elizabeth, and also Queen Anne, was "*Semper eadem,*"— "Always the same." The words "*Ich dien,*" in the German language, mean, "I serve." These were added to the arms of the Prince of Wales after the battle of Cressy, in which John, king of Bohemia, who was blind, was killed His crest was three ostrich feathers with the above motto, which Edward the Black Prince assumed in commemoration of his victory.

DISHES. Part of the payment of the king's servants used to consist of a certain number of dishes of meat. The lord president of the council was formerly allowed ten dishes of meat per diem These ten dishes were eventually compounded for at £1000 per annum, while his salary was only £500. The lord steward had sixteen dishes. At the installation of the Knights of the Garter, the knights were liberally provided. "On St. George's day, 1667, each knight" says Evelyn, "had forty dishes to his mess, piled up five or six high."

DIVING BELL. This was mentioned obscurely by Aristotle, about 325 B.C. The first diving bell was a very large kettle, suspended by ropes, with the mouth downwards,

58

and planks to sit on fixed in the middle of its concavity
Two Greeks at Toledo, in 1588, made an experiment before
the Emperor Charles V, when they descended in it with a
lighted candle to a considerable depth   It is said to have
been used on the coast of Mull, in searching for the wreck
of part of the Spanish Armada.   Smeaton made use of the
diving bell in improving Ramsgate harbour.   In 1683,
William Phipps, the son of a blacksmith, formed a project
for unloading a rich Spanish ship sunk on the coast of
Hispaniola   Charles II. gave him a ship with everything
necessary for his undertaking; but being unsuccessful, returned in great poverty.   He then endeavoured to procure
another vessel, but failing, projected a subscription, to which
the Duke of Albemarle contributed.   In 1687, Phipps set
sail in a ship of 200 tons, having previously engaged to
divide the profits according to the twenty shares of which
the subscription consisted.   At first all his labours proved
fruitless ; but at length he was fortunate enough to bring up
so much treasure, that he returned to England with the
value of £200,000 sterling.   Of this sum he got about
£20,000, and the duke £90,000.   Phipps was knighted by
the king, and laid the foundation of the fortunes of the
house of Mulgrave.   The *Royal George*, which went down
in 1782, was first surveyed by means of the diving bell, in
May, 1817, and since then it has been continually employed
in submarine surveys.

DOE, JOHN, AND RICHARD ROE.   In the trial
(on appeal) of Louis Houssart for the murder of his wife, in
1724, as usual, the names of John Doe and Richard Roe
were entered in the common form as pledges to prosecute.
Among other pleas in bar to and abatement of the proceed-

ings, Houssart pleaded, " that there were no such persons as John Doe and Richard Roe, who were mentioned as pledges in the appeal." To this it was replied, not that it was the usual form, but "that *there were* two such persons in Middle-sex as John Doe and Richard Roe—the one a weaver, and the other a soldier, and this fact was sworn to." This form seems, then, to have been considered, in this case, something more than a mere legal fiction, or there would not have been such a replication.

DOG DAYS. The explanation of this term, is those excessively hot days, from the 24th of July to the 15th of August. The ancient Romans and others believed that the great dog, or dog-star, which then rises and sets with the sun, was the cause of the heat, and at that season they always sacrificed a brown dog to Canicula, to appease its rage.

DOOMSDAY BOOK. This book was composed by order of William the Conqueror, and contains a register of every estate in England, with its value, the quality of the land, and an account of all the cattle, servants, and *slaves* belonging to it.

DRUMS This musical instrument is said to be of oriental invention, and was brought by the Arabians into Spain. The kettle-drum was so called because it resembled a large kettle or boiler standing upon three short legs.

DUCAT. The origin of ducats is referred to one Longinus, governor of Italy, who. revolting against the emperor, Justin the younger, made himself Duke of Ravenna, and called himself *Exarcha, i.e.* without lord or ruler, and to show his independence, struck pieces of money of very pure gold, in his own name, and with his own stamp, which were called *ducati*, hence the word ducats.

DUCKING-STOOL. This was another sort of punishment for such as were " famous for a scolding tongue " (see *Gossip's Bridle*). It is described as follows :—" A post was set up in a pond ; upon the former was placed a transverse beam, turning on a swivel, with a chair at one end of it." In this the scolding woman was placed, and the end turned to the pond, and let down into the water. Scolds were also punished by fines in the manorial courts.

DUDS-DAY FRIDAY. This is so called because of its being the first subsequent to the term of Whitsunday, and a market day on which the country people make their annual purchases of clothes. Penny reels used to be one of the principal amusements upon that day. To the annual returns the merchants of Kilmarnock look forward with anticipations of gain ; and in general they are not disappointed.

DUELLING. This reprehensible mode of settling disputes—now, happily, all but extinct—arose from the impression that, in single combat, Providence would not fail to declare itself in favour of the innocent. This custom is supposed to have been brought into Italy towards the end of the fifth century. In a short time it spread through Europe, and was very generally resorted to as a mode of settling disputes It was introduced into England by William the Conqueror, and in course of time became regularly recognised by the various governments, and elevated into a species of public trial. " Trial by battle " was

legalised till 1817, when the last appeal to arms took place ,
the law permitting it was abolished in 1819. In 1845 a
society was founded to discourage duelling.

DUKE. Among the Saxons, the Latin names of dukes
—*duces*—is very frequent, and signified among the Romans,
the commanders or leaders of their armies. In the laws of
Henry I. they are called *heretochii.* But after the Norman
Conquest, which changed the military polity of the nation,
the kings themselves continuing for many generations Dukes
of Normandy, they would not honour any subject with the
title before 1337. In the reign of Elizabeth, 1572, the
order became extinct; but it was revived about fifty years
afterwards, in the person of George Villiers, Duke of Buckingham.

DUKE HUMPHREY. The proverb of "dining with
Duke Humphrey" is thus explained. Humphrey, Duke of
Gloucester, was a man of great hospitality, and at his death
was buried in St. Paul's, hence it is said of those who walk
there during the time of dinner, that they are dining with
Duke Humphrey, which implies that they are unable to
procure a meal elsewhere.

DUN. Many have thought that the word *dun* was
derived from the French *donnez* (give me); but the true
origin of that name is from one John Dun, a famous bailiff
of the city of Lincoln, in Henry VII.'s reign . so extremely
active and dexterous was he in his profession, that it became
a common proverb when any unlucky wight could not or
would not pay, to say, "Why don't you Dun him?"

6

E.

EARL. This word—*eorle* in Saxon, *comes* Latin—was a great title among the Saxons, who termed them *ealdermen* —elder men—signifying the same as senior or senator among the Romans; and also *sciremen*, because they had each of them the civil government of a separate division or shire. On the irruption of the Danes, they changed the names to *eorles*, which signified the same in their language. The title of earl is the most ancient of the English peerage, there being no title of honour used by our present nobility that was likewise in use by the Saxons except this, which was usually applied to the first in the royal line; and anciently there was no earl but had a *shire* or county for his earldom.

EAST (Turning to the). The east, in scriptural language, was, symbolically considered, the more immediate residence of the Almighty, and has been emphatically alluded to in every age, although turning to the east savours, in some degree, of Catholicism, and even in the present day is one of the rites of that form of religion. The sun rises in the east, and the prophets of old always turned their faces in that direction when engaged in their devotions. A brilliant star appeared in the east at the birth of the Messiah. Balaam, Cyrus, and the Magi came from the east. It may be considered merely a sort of devotional piety. commanded to be observed by the canon law The Christian churches were anciently built due east and west, and in the early period of Christianity it was usual in Poland, Lithuania, and many other countries, when the creeds were read, for the nobility to rise up and stand facing the east, with their swords drawn, thereby intimating that they were ready, if necessary, to seal the truth of their belief with their blood and life.

EASTER. It is so called from *Eastre*, the goddess of the east, a Saxon deity, who was worshipped with great solemnity in the month of April. The Hebrews termed it *pasach*, which means to skip, or *pass over.* (See *Passover.*) Others think it originated from a Saxon word, meaning *to rise*, expressive of the resurrection of Christ. It was anciently called the great day, feast, or queen of feasts, as it governed all the other moveable feasts. Easter-day is the first Sunday following the first full moon after the 21st of March, and was so ordered by the Council of Nice in 325 There was, originally, a custom of beating and stoning Jews on this day.

EASTER DUES. These are " customary sums " which have been paid from time immemorial in the church, and are recoverable as small tithes before two justices of the peace. Before the time of Edward VI. *offering, oblations,* and *obventions* (one and the same thing), constituted the chief revenues of the church, and were collected at Christmas, Easter, Whitsuntide, and the Feast of the Dedication of the particular parish church ; but by an act passed in 1540, it was enacted that such offerings should thenceforth be paid at Easter—a law or rule which is reinforced by the rubric at the end of the Communion Service in our Book of Common Prayer.

EDINBURGH (The Dukedom of). This title, bestowed by her Majesty on her second son, Prince Alfred, deserves notice, and it may not be out of place to mention the connection of the Royal family with the peerage in ques-

64

tion. His Royal Highness Prince William Henry, son of Frederick Prince of Wales and brother of George III., was created, on the 19th of November, 1764, Duke of Gloucester and Edinburgh. The latter title was not used, though both were British peerages, the crown having had no power to create a Scottish peerage since the passing of the Act of Union on the 1st of May, 1707. The elder Duke of Gloucester and Edinburgh died in 1805, and was succeeded by his son, Prince William Frederick, at whose death, without issue, on the 30th November, 1834, the two peerages became extinct. The title of Duke of Edinburgh is therefore a new creation in favour of his Royal Highness Prince Alfred, and will be borne as his first title.

EGGS OF DIFFERENT COLOURS. Eggs of several birds are of various colours and differently spotted, because wild fowls live chiefly on insects, or those kinds of food which grow wild; but as almost all tame fowls live principally on corn, their eggs are usually of a white colour, though sometimes slightly tinged, which may, in some manner, be attributed to the nature and propensities of the birds.

ELECTRICITY. This word is derived from the Greek (see *Amber*); but, considered as a science, is of modern origin. William Gilbert, a physician in London in 1600, is the earliest writer on the subject, other authors followed at intervals; and in the year 1660 the first electrical machine was invented. This was gradually improved upon, and in 1744 it began to be used for medical purposes.

ELECTRIC TELEGRAPH. This invention was patented in 1837, and the idea is said to have originated with Mr. James Bain. The practical application is due to Messrs. Cooke and Wheatstone. The first electric telegraph was laid down upon the London and Blackwall Railway ; the second, from London to West Drayton; the third, from London to Gosport.

EMBALMING. Among the ancient Egyptians, it was believed that as long as the body was kept from corruption, the soul hovered near it, and would ultimately reanimate it in its original form; but if the deceased were known to be guilty of any crime, his body was not allowed to be embalmed or buried. They also believed that after the lapse of 36,000 years the soul would re-inhabit the body ; hence their practice of embalming. One of the substances for embalming was a sort of wax, which, in the Arabic language, is called *mum*, from which is derived the English term, mummy. They also embalmed the bodies of those animals they held sacred, such as the monkey, lion, crocodile, bear, rat, dog, cat, wolf, etc.

EMBER WEEKS, are those four seasons set apart for public ordinations, particularly for prayer and fasting, namely : the first week in Lent, the next after Whitsunday, the 24th of September, and 13th of December. They were so called from the practice of sprinkling dust or embers on the head, in token of humiliation.

EMBLEMENTS. In law, a term used for the produce of land sown or planted by a tenant for life or years, whose estate is determined suddenly after the land is sown or planted, and before harvest.

EMBROIDERY. The art of working upon cloth with the needle, and embroidering figures of various kinds with

66

different coloured threads, is of very ancient date, having been taught by the Egyptians to the Israelites. The Anglo-Saxon ladies were so famed for their skill in this art, that their productions were highly esteemed in foreign countries, and called by way of eminence, the " English work." At first, threads exceedingly massive were employed for weaving and embroidery; and large tassels, the threads of which are of pure gold, have been discovered at Herculaneum.

EMERY. There is a curious Rabbinical tradition connected with this substance. Moses is said to have engraved the stones of the Rationale with the blood of the worm " samir." When Solomon was about to build the temple with stones untouched by the tool, he inclosed an ostrich chick in a glass vase. The mother ostrich, wishing to release her offspring, fled to the desert and brought a supply of the worm " samir," which the sagacious monarch used for his own purposes. Now, as emery was called by the Greeks *smyris*, it is pretty evident that the magical worm was neither more nor less than that mineral.

EMPEROR. This word is derived from the Latin *imperator*, a title given by the Romans to successful generals, and afterwards assumed by the heads of the state. In modern times it applies a title of dignity superior to that of king. The " kingdom " of France was created an " empire " by the first Napoleon, who annexed to it Belgium and Italy, and the present emperor only follows prudently in the steps .of his uncle. Queen Victoria, however, if there is any meaning in titles, is more truly an Empress than Napoleon is an Emperor, for she governs a third of the habitable

F 2

globe, and rules over sixty or seventy different dependencies. (See *King.*)

EMPIRE   This is usually a territory of greater extent than a kingdom, which may be, and often is, a territory of small extent. Thus we say, the Russian empire; the Austrian empire; the British empire.

EMPIRES (Renowned). The most conspicuous empires in history are the Assyrian, Persian, Grecian, and Roman; but several others have been equally famous, such as the Egyptian, Parthian, Chinese, etc. The most renowned nations of antiquity are now of little note or importance, as Greece, Asia Minor, Palestine, Egypt, Italy, etc.; whilst the most barbarous nations of antiquity, are now the most polished and civilized, as Albion, Gallia, Belgium, Helvetia, etc., now called Britain, France, Netherlands, Switzerland, etc.

ENGLAND. This word is derived from *Angles,* a tribe of Germans who settled in Britain. These joined the Saxon adventurers, a people of North Germany, who were invited over to assist the Britons in their wars against the Picts, and who eventually became masters of the kingdom. The Scots received their names from Scoti, a colony from Ireland. The Picts were a Gothic colony from Norway, and received the name of Caledonians, Caledonia being the ancient name of Scotland.

ENGLISH TOWNS. Many of our ancient towns derive their names from the Saxon, and were called according to their locality,—thus, a great number end in *combe,* such as Ilfracombe, Yarcombe, etc. Combe signifies a valley beneath two hills, or a valley with trees on each side. Others end in *minster*, which means a monastery or conventual church. Others end in *mouth*, which signifies the mouth of the river near or on which the town stands. *Ton* implies a hill, hedge, or wall. *Wyke*, *wick*, or *wich*, means a village, castle, or bay. *Burgh* means borough. *Ham*, a house, farm, or village. *Chester*, from the Latin *castrum*, a castle or tower on the highway. *Bury*, a dwelling-place or house. *Ford*, a shallow part of a river. *Port*, a place or harbour for ships. *Pool*, a large collection of deep and standing water, supported by springs *Hurst*, a little wood or thicket of trees, or orchard *Wald* or *wold*, a forest. *Burn* or *brune*, a river, ford, or brook.

ENGINES (Fire). The ancients are supposed to have extinguished their conflagrations by the aid of some hydraulic machine. The modern kind of fire-engine is first noticed as having been used at the city of Augsburg, in 1518. In 1699, a patent was taken out in Paris for an implement of this description. The introduction of the fire-engine into England very probably occurred about the year 1650.

ENGRAVING. The invention of this beautiful art is said to be due to the Egyptians. Originally it was practised upon precious stones. From the Egyptians it became known to the Greeks and Romans, and by the latter probably introduced into Britain. In the reign of Alfred the Great, the Anglo-Saxon goldsmiths were the principal engravers. From the time of the Crusades, Europe was acquainted with a method of engraving from which ink might have been delivered, and copies multiplied ; yet it was not till about 1437 that any one thought of procuring impressions in this way. The Italians, Germans, and Dutch, contest the honour of this discovery. The invention of

69

engraving on copper plates is generally ascribed to Muso Finiguerra, a goldsmith of Florence, about 1460. Impressions from plates, it is said, were first taken in England in 1540. Etching, or engraving on copper-plate by means of aqua fortis, was invented by Albert Durer, a German, in 1511, and introduced into England in the time of Charles I.

ENIGMA. The use of enigmas is exceedingly ancient; their construction and solution constituted a very common amusement, and, in some cases, an important occupation among the nations of antiquity. The kings of Egypt and Babylon sent riddles to one another for solution. Solomon and Hiram kept up a correspondence of a similar kind, in which, we are assured by Josephus, the former had always the advantage. The Greeks proposed riddles to their guests; but the Romans took little interest in such matters. Many ancient riddles have come down to us; the one proposed by Samson to the Philistines (Jud. xiv. 14) is of course well known. Also that proposed to Œdipus by the Sphynx, " What animal goes in the morning on four feet, at noon on two, and in the evening on three ?" The answer to which was, " Man—who crawls when a child, walks when mature, and is supported by a stick in old age."

EPIPHANY. This means an appearance of great light, a festival celebrated twelve days after Christmas, as our Saviour was manifested to the Gentiles by a miraculous blazing star.

EPITAPHS. These are of much more ancient date than tombstones, as we find the Athenians used to place a kind of scroll over the burying-place of the dead, with the name inscribed, and the word, Good, Hero, etc., expressive of their opinions. The Lacedemonians would only allow epitaphs to those who died in battle. The Romans inscribed epitaphs to the spirits of the defunct ; but in the present day they are generally of a fulsome nature, attributing virtues to the deceased which they never possessed whilst living.

EQUINOX. When the sun in his progress passes through the equator in one of the equinoctial points, the day and night are equal all over the globe. This occurs twice in the year ; about March 21, the *vernal* equinox, and September 22, the *autumnal* equinox. The equinoctial points move backwards about 50 seconds yearly, requiring 25,000 years to accomplish a complete revolution. This is called the procession of the equinoxes, which is said to have been observed by the ancient astronomers.

ERRORS (Vulgar). The following is a list of popular errors, many of which were once firmly believed in, and some of which survive, even now .—That when a man designs to marry a woman who is in debt, if he take her from the priest clothed only in her under garment, he will not be liable for her engagements. That there was no land tax before the reign of William III. That if a criminal be hung an hour, and revives, he cannot be afterwards executed. That a funeral passing over any place makes a public highway. That a husband has the power of divorcing his wife by selling her in open market with a halter round her neck. That second cousins may not marry, though first cousins may. That it is necessary in some legal process against the reigning sovereign, to go through the fiction of arresting him, which is done by placing a ribbon across the road, as if to impede the carriage. That

71

the lord of a manor may shoot over all the lands within his manor. That pounds of butter may be of any number of ounces. That "bull-beef" shall not be sold, unless the bull has been baited previously to being killed. That leases are made for the term of 999 years, because a lease of 1,000 years would create a freehold. That deeds executed on a Sunday are void. That in order to disinherit an heir-at-law, it is necessary to give him a shilling by the will; for that otherwise he would be entitled to the whole property.

ESQUIRE. Some people suppose that any gentleman in the possession of property, value £300 per annum, may use the title, but this supposition is erroneous. We often see it applied, as a matter of courtesy, to rich merchants, opulent tradesmen, and people who live on their own private property; but strictly speaking, it is only applicable to the eldest sons of viscounts, lords, younger sons of noblemen and their heirs, elder sons of knights, baronets, Knights of the Bath and their heirs; also those who serve the monarch in any worshipful calling or public office in the kingdom, such as high sheriff, justice of the peace (whilst he holds his commission), coroners, and Masters in Chancery. The eldest sons of peers in Great Britain are only esquires in terms of law, although they are termed lords. If the monarch puts spurs on the heels of any gentleman, and a collar marked SS. on his neck, he is reckoned an esquire.

ESTATE. This word, as used in law, is nearly synonymous with "interest." Thus we say a person has a "life estate," meaning that he is entitled to the enjoyment of land, of house, etc., during his life, but that he cannot bequeath it, and that on his death it will not descend to his heirs.

ETERNITY. We cannot understand anything about this word, as it is far beyond human comprehension. A finite being cannot comprehend infinity; and as the faculties and powers of man are limited, he can no more describe the word than he can ascertain the mysteries, designs, and intentions of Providence. This word is so indefinite, that it is mentioned but once in the Bible : by the prophet Isaiah, chapter lvii. verse 15. It was once asked, "Suppose the whole globe were converted into a mass of sand, and one grain of it exhausted every thousand years, in what space of time would the whole be annihilated?" The answer was, *never*, which last word is as far above our comprehension as eternity itself.

EUROPEAN NATIONS. (Names of.) These are derived principally from some particular cause or object. For instance, *Ireland* (which Julius Cæsar first called Hibernia) is a kind of modification of Erin, or the country of the west. *Scotland*, from Scotia, a tribe which originally came from Ireland. It was anciently called Caledonia, which means a mountainous country, forests, and lands. *Portugal*, the ancient Lusitania, was so named from a town on the river Douro, called Cale, opposite to which the inhabitants built a city called Porto, or Oporto; and when the country was recovered from the Moors, the inhabitants combined the words, and called it the kingdom of Portucale—hence Portugal. *Spain* (the ancient Iberia, from the river Iberus), or Hispania, from the Phœnician Spaniga, which signifies abounding with rabbits, which animals are very numerous in that country—hence Spain. *France*, from the Franks, a people of Germany, who conquered that country. Its ancient name was Celta, Gaul, or Gallia-Bracchata, the latter signifying striped breeches, which were worn by the natives. *Switzerland*, the ancient Helvetia, was so named by the Austrians, who called all the inhabitants of these mountainous countries Schweitzers. *Italy* received its present name from a renowned prince called Italus. It was called Hesperia, from its western locality. *Holland*, the ancient Batavi, a warlike people, was so named from the German word *hohl*, the English of which is hollow, implying a very low country. The inhabitants are called Dutch, from the German deutsch, or teutsch. *Sweden* and *Norway* were anciently called Scandinavia, which the northern antiquarians think means a country the woods of which had been burnt or destroyed. The appellation, Sweden, is derived from Sictuna, or Suitheod. The native term, Norway, or the northern way, explains itself. *Prussia*, from Pruzzi, a Sclavonic race; but some writers suppose it took its name from Russia, and the Sclavonic syllable *po*, which means adjacent, or near. *Denmark* means the marches, territories, or boundaries of the Danes. *Russia* is the ancient Sarmatia, which has been subsequently named Moscovy. It derived its present name from Russi, a Sclavonic tribe, who founded the Russian monarchy; the original savage inhabitants used to paint their bodies, in order to appear more terrible in battle. They generally lived in the mountains, and their chariots were their only habitations. *Turkey* took its name from the Turks, or Turcomans, which signifies wanderers, and originally belonged to the Scythians or Tartars. It is sometimes called the Ottoman Empire, from Othoman, one of their principal leaders

71

EVANGELISTS (The). *St. Matthew*, whose original name was Levi, was a Jew of the tribe of Issachar; he was a publican, or tax-gatherer, and whilst sitting at the receipt of customs, was called by the Saviour to follow Him. He preached the gospel throughout Judæa, and whilst employed in this pious cause in Ethiopia, he was slain with a halbert. *St. Mark*, whose original name was Mordecai, was also of Jewish parents, and was converted to Christianity by some of the apostles. He preached the gospel principally in Egypt; and whilst the Egyptians were employed in their heathen solemnities, they broke in upon the holy man, who was worshipping his God, bound his feet with cords, and dragged him through the streets till he died. *St. Luke* was supposed to have been a physician, also an eminent painter, and was converted to the Christian faith by St. Paul, with whom he preached the gospel; but was seized at Patras, in Achaia, by a party of infidels, who hung him to an olive-tree, in the eighty-fourth year of his age. *St. John* was a disciple of Christ, and spread the gospel through western Asia. He addressed himself to the seven Churches mentioned in the book of Revelation, and converted thousands to Christianity. By order of Domitian, the Roman emperor, he was thrown into a cauldron of boiling oil, from which he came out, not only unhurt, but greatly refreshed, after which he was banished to the Isle of Patmos, where he wrote the Revelation. He died a natural death at Ephesus, in the ninety-fourth year of his age.

EVIL MAY-DAY. Was so called on account of the violence of the apprentices and the populace against foreigners, especially the French, May 1st, 1517.

EXCISE. A tax upon the commodities forming the

75

necessaries of life, was first resorted to by the Romans in the time of Augustus. The Earl of Bedford recommended a similar tax to Charles I., but it was not carried into effect till the year 1643, when it first took the name of excise.

F.

FAIR AUCTION. A singular custom prevails among the young rustics on the banks of the Eiffel, on the north-eastern frontier of France. On the morning of St. Matthew's day, they collect together from the several villages, and put up the whole maiden portion of the community to auction, calling out the name of every lass in succession, and knocking her down to the highest bidder. The fortunate purchaser, in right of his acquisition, is entitled to become her *cavaliere servente* for the next six months. In other districts the youths draw lots, when they plant the May-tree, for the maidens of their respective villages, and each of them becomes, for one twelvemonth afterwards, the sweetheart elect of the damsel whose name he has drawn. If she marry, and he has not previously renounced his right, she enjoys the privilege of calling upon him to give her a good character.

FAIRIES. The popular faith in fairies has existed in England for all ages ; and they are by far the most interesting of all the mythological personages, a belief in whom was once an article in every popular creed. Chaucer tells us that in the days of King Arthur—

> " The elf-queen, with her jolly company,
> Danced full oft in many a greenè mead."

And some trace the opinions relative to fairies to the tradi-

76

tions derived from the Druidical superstitions. That the aboriginal Britons believed in fairies appears highly probable, from the similarity of character observable between the sprites of England and those of Wales and Ireland. But whether they did or not, "our Saxon ancestors," as Dr. Percy observes, long before they left their German forests, believed in the existence of a kind of diminutive demon, or middle species between men and spirits, whom they called *dwerger*, or dwarfs.

FAIRS. Fairs and feasts were formerly held in churchyards, in honour of the saint to whom the church was dedicated; but in consequence of their being very much abused, they were finally suppressed, according to Spelman, in the thirteenth of Edward III., as appears by the following xtract :—" And the Kynge commandeth and forbiddeth that from henceforth, neither fairs and markets shall be kept in churchyards, for the honour of the church. Given at Westminster, the viii. of Octobre, the xiii. yeare of Kynge Edwarde's reigne."

FAIRY RINGS. By fairy rings is meant a phenomenon common in the fields, and which are supposed by the vulgar in England, to be traced by the fairies in their dances— hence the appellation. There are two kinds of fairy rings, one of about seven yards in diameter, containing a round bare path, a foot broad, with grass in the middle of it; the other is smaller in size, encompassed by a circumference of grass, greener and fresher than that of the middle. Some attribute them to the effects of lightning, but they are now known to result from the outspreading propagation of a particular agaric, or mushroom, by which the ground is manured for a richer following vegetation.

FAN.   This is a very ancient apparatus, having been used from the remotest times by the ladies of Egypt and India, as well as those of modern times, for cooling the face, etc., by agitating the air.   Fans were originally made of feathers bound together, like the tail of a peacock when spread out.

FEE-SIMPLE.   A person is said to have the fee-simple of a piece of land or a house, when he has the entire, absolute, and unconditional ownership of it; and when, if he were to die intestate, it might be inherited not only by his descendants, but by his relations generally, according to the ruler of inheritance and succession prescribed by law.

FEE-TAIL.   Is an estate in land granted to a man and the heirs of his body.   It descends only to the issue of the person who first takes the land, and if they fail, it becomes the property of the heir of the person who first granted it. Each person who successively comes into possession of such an estate, is called a "tenant-in-tail," and except by a peculiar conveyance, enrolled in the Court of Chancery, he cannot alienate it, so as to deprive the heir of his right to inherit it.

FELT.   There is a curious tradition respecting the discovery of this material, which, though rather odd, is not in reality more so than the origin of numerous other articles of ordinary use.   It is, that while Clement IV., Bishop of Rome, was flying from his persecutors, his feet became blistered, in consequence of which he was induced to put wool between the soles of his feet and the sandals which he wore.   The consequence was, that by the perspiration and the motion of his feet the wool became completely "felted," as if wrought expressly.   When he afterwards settled in

78

Rome he turned the discovery to use; and hence, it is said, the origin of felt-making.

FENIAN. This word has two derivations; the first is from the name of the ancient Irish chief, Fian; the second is from the Phœnix Club, a select society which existed in Ireland for many years.

FINGERS (Five). Our ancestors had distinct names for each of the five fingers, the thumb being generally called a finger in old works. The following were the cognomens, in order, viz.—*Thumb, toucher, long-man, leche-man,* and *little-man* In a MS. quoted in Halliwell's "Dictionary of Archaisms," the reasons for the names are thus given. The first finger was called *toucher,* because "therewith men touch, I wis." The second finger, *long-man,* "for longest finger it is." The third finger was called *leche-man,* because a leche, or doctor, tasted everything by means of it. We find elsewhere another reason for this appellation—the pulsation in it, which was at one time supposed to communicate direct with the heart. The other was, of course, called *little-man,* because it was the least of all. It is rather curious that some of these names should be still preserved in a nursery rhyme. Yet such is the fact, for one thus commences (the fingers being kept in corresponding movement) :—

> " Dance, Thumkin, dance,
> Dance, ye merry men, every one ;
> Thumkin he can dance alone,
> Thumkin he can dance alone."

And so on for four more verses, taking each finger in succession, and naming the *fore-man, long-man, ring-man,* and *little man.*

79

FIRE AND WATER (Ordeal by).   This was a mode of trial common among the ancient Greeks, and was in use in England until abolished by Henry III.   The ordeal by fire was confined to the upper class of people, that of water to the lower, hence the expression "going through fire and water to serve another;" these being allowed to be performed by deputy.

FIREARMS.   The first mention of portable firearms is in connection with the garrison of Lucca, when besieged by the Florentines, in 1430.   The new kind of weapon consisted of a club of a cubit and a half long, having at one end an iron barrel, or small cannon, which the besieged carried in their hands.   Hand-guns, or "hange-gunnes," as they were called, of a description somewhat similar to the above, were used by the English soldiers about the year 1460, having been introduced by some Flemings in the service of Edward IV.

FIREWORKS.   The Chinese are said to be the inventors of these ingenious productions.   In England they are first mentioned as being applied to the public rejoicing at the marriage of Henry VIII. with Anne Boleyn.

FISH (Gold).   The beautiful little fish, called in this country "gold and silver fish," were originally natives of China and Japan, where they are held in great estimation, and are called *kuyn.*   From China the English carried some of them to the island of St. Helena, and from thence the captain of one of our East India ships brought some of them to England, in the year 1788.

FISH AND THE RING.   The Eastern tale of "The Fish and the Ring," invented thousands of years since, has

8ɟ

survived to our own day, and is still related and believed. But there is only one authenticated instance. In the church at Stepney is a tomb to the memory of Lady Rebecca Berry, who died 1696, in whose coat of arms a fish and an amulet appear. She has hence been supposed to be the heroine of a once popular ballad, the scene of which is laid in York-shire, entitled " The Cruel Knight ; or, Fortunate Farmer's Daughter," which narrates how one of knightly rank, in passing a village, heard the cry of a woman in travail, and was told by a witch that he was doomed to marry the child then born on her arrival at womanhood. The knight, in deep dis-gust, draws a ring from his finger, and casting it into a rapid river, vows he will never do so unless she can produce that ring. After many years a fish is brought to the farmer's daughter to dress for dinner, and she finds the ring in its stomach, enabling her to win a titled husband, who no longer fights against his fate.

FIXING THE HORSESHOE. At Lancaster, at the junction of four of the principal streets, is fixed a horseshoe, which is renewed every seventh year, with certain cere-monies, in remembrance of John of Gaunt's horse losing a shoe there, which was picked up and fixed in the wall.

FLAGS AND SIGNALS. Red, white, yellow, and blue are the most conspicuous colours. The present French tricolour—red, white, and blue—is a good example of the effect produced by the simplest possible combination of three colours in the same flag. Our royal standard has a groundwork in some parts red and in others blue, with yellow or golden lions, and harps, and so forth. Our admiralty flag has a yellow anchor on a red ground. Our Union Jack has a blue ground, red rectangular stripes, and white diagonals. Our red and blue admiral's flags are plain. Many of the other English flags have a plain ground colour over five-sixths of the surface, with a cross of stripes in one corner In most of the nations of Europe, the colours on the naval flags are generally red, white (or yellow), and blue. Even his Holiness the Pope has one flag with a white lamb and a white cross on a red ground; and another with a yellow St. Peter on a red ground. King Bomba, of Naples, had a yellow griffin on a white ground. Hamburgh has a white castle on a red ground. Venice has an amiable-looking yellow lion on a red ground, holding a yellow sword in one paw, and a white book in another, and Bremen has a sort of red and white chess-board, with six times nine squares instead of eight times eight.

FLAP JACK In former times, on Shrove Tuesday, when the people were denied meat, they had recourse to fritters, which being composed of flour, eggs, and spice, and fried in a pan, was called "Flap Jack;" this we now call pancake.

FLAPPING AND BABBLING. A singular custom was annually observed at Ottringham, a village of Middle Holderness, about seven miles from Hedon. This took place on the eve of November 5th, and consisted in what was called flapping the church; to do which, the lads in the parish, each having provided himself with a cord to which was attached a stout piece of leather about six inches long, proceeded to the church, headed by the parish clerk. Being all assembled in the church, which was lighted up for the occasion, the ringers commenced a peal, and then began the flapping. The clerk having called out, "Now, boys, flap away," directly all the pews in the church were assailed, inside and out, by the flappers. Having thrashed

the pews for some time, the leathern missiles were generally
at the finish directed against each other; and the whole
ceremony ended with a regular steeple-chase throughout the
sacred edifice. At Roos, in Middle Holderness, was a
similar custom, called " Babbling." Also at Skulaugh, in
North Holderness, this ceremony of flapping or babbling
was yearly observed.

FLEUR DE LIS. This beautiful flower, called also
the iris, is a native of France, and is generally placed in
maps to denote the northern point of the mariner's compass.
It was so placed by the inventor of the compass, out of
compliment to France, it being a part of the arms of the
king of that country, and also used in the embellishments
of the crown itself. Edward III. added the fleur de lis to
the arms of England, but since the union with Ireland, it has
given place to the shamrock.

FLITCH OF BACON. The ceremony of presenting
a gammon, or flitch, of bacon to any married couple who
took an oath "that he or she has been married a year
and a day, without quarrelling or repenting, and that, if
they were then single, and wished to be married again, the
demandant would take the same party before any other in
the world," is first mentioned as having been established
at Whichnor, Essex, in 1338, by the lord of the manor of
Dunmow, Sir Philip de Somerville. The earliest recorded
delivery of the bacon was in 1444, and the last, August 16th,
1869. It is, however, very strange, that twelve couples
only, during 500 years, dared to swear they deserved a flitch
of bacon for the undisturbed calmness of their matrimonial
life.

83

FLORA DAY A remarkable festival was formerly held in the town of Helston, on the 8th of May, called "Helston Flora Day," when all business was suspended, and the inhabitants went forth into the country, with music, singing, and dancing, where they adorned themselves with garlands of flowers, and returning to the town, spent the rest of the day in songs, feasting, and merriment. This is supposed to have been a relic of the old Roman festival in honour of Flora; and although it has changed its features in some respects, the day is still kept as a holiday.

FLOTSAM This means when a ship is broken up and goods float upon the water between high and low water marks. *Jetsam* is when the ship is in danger of foundering, and the goods are cast into the sea for the purpose of saving it. *Ligam* is when heavy goods are thrown into the sea with a buoy, to be found again. If no owner claims them within one year and a day, they belong to the crown.

FLOWERING SUNDAY. A very pretty custom prevails in the country districts of South Wales, of assembling in the churchyards, on Palm Sunday, and spreading fresh flowers upon the graves of friends and relatives. This custom is not by any means confined to the lower classes, and in many of the graveyards, flowers of hot-house culture are mingled with the more modest field flowers.

FLUTE. This instrument was known to the Greeks and Romans, who were devotedly attached to its dulcet sounds. It derives its name from *fluta*, the classical name for the lamprey, because, like that fish, it is long and perforated along the side.

94

FOLIO, &c. Fol. or folio, implies that the book is printed on single sheets of paper, once folded down, which of course, makes it of the largest size : 4to or quarto, means four leaves to the sheet, or a sheet twice doubled : 8vo or octavo, implies eight leaves to the sheet, or a sheet folded four times. Twelve leaves, or 24 pages, make a duodecimo, or 12mo; 16 leaves, or 32 pages, a 16mo; 18 leaves, or 36 pages, an 18mo ; 24 leaves, or 48 pages, a 24mo.

FOOD (Native). Every nation has its peculiar taste. The Abyssinians cut a slice from a living ox, and esteem it one of their chief delicacies. The Tartars think horse-flesh their greatest dainty. The Greenlanders and Samoi-edes think train oil the finest of all sauces to their dried fish or flesh, and are able to digest a full meal of whale's fat. Cats were eaten in Spain, and their mistresses compelled to confine them, lest they should be stolen for human food. The French have a great partiality for frogs and snails ; and a dish of the latter was very common at a Roman table. The English are noted for their partiality to roast beef. The Egyptians abhor fish, and it has been known that the Neapolitans refused potatoes when there was a famine.

FOOL (Lord-Mayor's). In some ancient works a jester is described as " a witty and jocose person, kept by princes to inform them of their faults, and those of other men, under the disguise of a waggish story " Several of our ancient kings, particularly the Tudors, kept jesters. Rayhere, the founder of St. Bartholomew's priory, Smithfield, is said to have been a court-jester and minstrel. There was a jester at court in the reigns of James I. and Charles I.,

85

but we hear of no licensed jester afterwards. The lord-mayor's fool is also now among the things of the past.

FOOLSCAP. The origin of this name for certain kinds of writing paper is explained thus :—The kings of England, before the reign of Charles I., monopolized the manufacture of this useful article. After this monarch was beheaded, all monopolies were swept away from the crown ; and in this particular case, by way of showing their contempt for this monarch, the Parliament directed the royal arms (watermark) to be taken from the paper, substituting a fool, with his cap and bells.

FOOTBALL. The custom of kicking a football through the streets for several hours on Shrove Tuesday has prevailed in Kingston and Teddington, and many other places, from time immemorial. It is hoped, however, that this riotous practice will soon be discontinued. The custom formerly existed at Hampton, but has ceased there during the past eight or nine years.

FORKS. Neither the Greeks nor the Romans used forks. It was customary with them to have their food cut up into small pieces before it was served up, and they divided it with instruments called *ligulæ*, closely resembling our spoons. The use of forks was first known in Italy towards the end of the fifteenth century. In France they were entirely new at the termination of the sixteenth century. Coryat, an Englishman, who had travelled in Italy, is said to have introduced forks into England in 1610 ; and for doing so he met with considerable ridicule. In a word, the use of forks at table was at first considered as a superfluous luxury. In that case they were confined to convents, as was the case in regard to the congregation of St. Maur. At the present day they are not used in the East.

FOUNTAINS. Formerly, when the supply of water within houses was comparatively unknown, every leading street in London, and every town in the provinces, had its fountain, or conduit. It is worth noticing that these were more generally ornamented with a lion's head than with any other effigy. This symbol was adopted by the ancients, from the circumstance that the inundation of the Nile happened during the progress of the sun in Leo (the lion).

FOUR AGES. These are taken from the celebrated dream of Nebuchadnezzar, which was interpreted by the prophet Daniel. The head was *gold*, the body and arms *silver*, the thighs *brass*, and the legs *iron*. The golden age denotes Adam and Eve's innocence in the garden of Eden, where they had everything provided without labour. The silver age, in scriptural language, shows the effects of the sin of Adam and Eve, which were labour and sorrow. The brazen age denotes the corruption and wickedness of mankind, which arrived at such a height that the Almighty determined to destroy the world by a flood. The iron age means the wars which are perpetually carried on among mankind, when violence, oppression, rapine, and every species of crime spread over the earth.

FRENCH TRICOLOUR. The origin of the tricolour is thus stated. In 1789, after the defection of the French Guards, a permanent committee of electors sat at six electoral halls, for the purpose of providing arms and provisions for the people. It was determined to raise a city guard of 40,000 men, each district to contribute a battalion of 800. The name of the guard was the "Parisian Militia," their colours, *blue* and *red*, were mixed with the *white* of their friends—the *Garde Française.* The Parisian militia became the "National Guard," and their colours the *tricolour*, from this union or "fraternisation."

FRIDAY (Unlucky.) The idea of Friday being an unlucky day originated in its being the day of the Crucifixion. Richard Cœur de Leon was killed on a Friday, which strengthened the superstition in the English mind.

FROGS OF NEGROLAND (or Nigritia, a large country in the interior of Africa). These are much larger than those of Europe, and make a great noise in the night, which, at a distance, very much resembles a pack of hounds in full cry. This is called a frog concert.

FRUIT (Native English). The only native fruits of this island are the strawberry, whortleberry, bilberry, cranberry, blackberry, wild plum, sloe, elderberry, yewberry, acorn, hips and haws, and very few others. But we have now almost every other kind of delicious fruit brought from abroad. Most of our best apples are supposed to have been introduced into Britain by a fruiterer of Henry VIII Matthew Paris, describing the bad season of 1257, observes that "apples were scarce, and pears scarcer, while quinces, cherries, plums, and all shell-fruits were entirely destroyed."

FUNERAL LOAVES. A singular custom is said to prevail at Gainsborough, of giving away penny loaves on the morning of a funeral, to whoever may demand them. This custom has prevailed for so long a period that the poorer inhabitants look upon it as a right.

88

G.

GALVANISM. Galvanism was first discovered at Bologna, 1791, by the lady of Louis Galvani, an Italian philosopher of great merit, and professor of anatomy—indeed, from whom the science received its name. His wife being possessed of a penetrating understanding, and devotedly attached to her husband, took a very lively interest in the science which at that period so much occupied his attention. At the time the incident we are about to narrate took place, she was in a declining state of health, and taking soup made of frogs by way of restorative. Some dead frogs happened to be lying on the table of Galvani's laboratory, where also stood an electrical machine, when the point of a knife was unintentionally brought into contact with the nerves of one of the frog's legs, which lay close to the conductor of the machine, and immediately the muscles of the limb were violently agitated. Madame Galvani having closely observed the phenomenon, instantly informed her husband of it ; and this incident led to the interesting discoveries which will transmit his name to the latest posterity.

GARDENS (Kitchen). Before the era of kitchen gardens, scurvy was one of the diseases by which the English population was kept down. Cabbages were not known in England until the period of Henry VIII. George I. was obliged to send to Holland to procure a lettuce for his queen. The Greeks and Romans took the cabbage as a remedy for the languor following inebriation.

GARTER (Order of the). An order of knighthood, instituted by Edward III. in consequence, it is supposed, of the Countess of Salisbury dropping her garter whilst dancing, which the king handed to her with the expression, "*Honi soit qui mal y pense;*" and observing some of his friends smile, he declared that many of those who laughed should soon be proud of wearing the garter; on which he created the order, the knights of which wear a blue riband, or garter.   Another account is that Edward imitated the celebrated King Arthur, by the order of the round table ; but as a number of foreign warriors crowded to him, the French king, with whom Edward was at war, instituted an order of his own, which soon procured him a like number of warriors ; but having violated the laws of hospitality, by seizing some English lords, Edward was so provoked, that he cried, "*Honi soit qui mal y pense,*" and converted the round table into the order of the garter, because at the battle of Cressy, where he defeated the French king, he fixed his garter on the end of his lance as a signal for the engagement.

GAWDY DAYS.   The derivation of the word Gawdy, may be taken from Judge Gawdy, who, it is believed, was the first institutor of those days ; or rather from *gaudium*, because they are days of joy, as bringing good cheer to the hungry students.   In colleges they are commonly called Gawdy, in inns of court Grand Days, and in some other places Collar Days.

(St) GEORGE'S (Day).   This is the twenty-third of April, and as almost every nation has its patron, or tutelary saint, St. George was selected for that of the English nation. It was supposed that he was born of English parents, and in early life became a good Christian.   He was greatly respected by the Emperor Diocletian, who gave him the command of a legion ; but he incurred the emperor's dis-

pleasure by the protection he afforded the Christians in their persecutions, and after having suffered the most grievous tortures, he was beheaded at Lydda, in 290. Various legends have resulted from his extraordinary prowess, such as his combat with the dragon, to preserve a princess from being devoured. This is typically represented on some of our current coins. In 1344 this day was made memorable by the creation of the Noble Order of St. George, or the Blue Garter; and there are many foreign knightly orders bearing his name.

GEMS (Alphabet of). The following alphabet may prove useful, as a name or a sentiment is formed by the arrangement of gems round the hoop of a ring, the initial letter of each gem employed forming words when combined :—

A—methyst—Agate.	N—icolo—Natralite.
B—eryl—Brilliant.	O—nyx—Opal.
C—halcedony—Chrysolite.	P—lasma—Pearl.
D—iamond.	Q—uirinus.
E—merald.	R—uby.
F—(*Pas de pierre connuc*).	S—apphire—Sardonyx.
G—arnet.	T—opaz—Turquois.
H—yacinth.	U—raine—Uworrovitz.*
I—ris.	V—ermeille—Verd antique.
J—asper—Jacinth.	W—(*Pas de pierre connue*).
K—(*Pas de pierre connue*).	X—epherene.
L—apis lazuli.	Y—(*Pas de pierre connue*).
M—alachite.	Z—amech.

GIPSIES. They were generally supposed to have descended from the Egyptians, one of the first people who pretended to foretell events, as related in the Bible, when Moses requested from Pharaoh the liberation of the

---

* A new Russian gem, called after a prince of that name.

Israelites.   The earliest account we have of them in
England was in 1530, when they were driven hence by
Henry VIII.   In the reign of Charles I. thirteen persons
were executed at one assize for having associated with
them, contrary to the statute.   Notwithstanding their in-
tercourse with other nations, they are still, like the Jews,
in their manners, customs, visage, and appearance, almost
wholly unchanged.   They have a peculiar language of their
own, which appears to be a compound of the most ancient
languages in the world.   The Bible has been translated
into the gipsy dialect.   Borrow says : " They generally style
themselves and their language ' Rommany,' and this word
is of Sanscrit origin, signifying ' the husband,' or that which
pertaineth unto them."   Again he observes : " Their coun-
tenances exhibit a decided family resemblance, but are
darker or fairer, according to the temperature of the climate
in which they dwell."   Their first recorded appearance was
in 1517.   They first visited Bohemia—hence the name
" Bohemians," given them by the French—and soon spread
over the rest of the continent.

GIVING QUARTER.   This phrase is said to have
originated from an agreement between the Dutch and
Spaniards, that the ransom of an officer or soldier should be
a quarter of his pay.   Hence to beg quarter, was to offer a
quarter of their pay for their safety, and to refuse quarter
was not to accept that composition as a ransom.

GIVING THE SACK.   One of the most comical
combats in the history of love, took place in the reign of
Maximilian II.   Two noblemen, one a German the other a
Spaniard, who had each rendered great service to the
emperor asked the hand of Helena, his daughter, in

9²

marriage. Maximilian replied, " That as he esteemed them both alike, it was impossible for him to choose between them, and that, therefore, their own prowess must decide it , but not being willing to risk the loss of either by engaging them in deadly combat, he ordered a large sack to be brought, and declared that he who should put his rival into it should have his fair Helena." And this whimsical combat was actually performed in the presence of the imperial court, and lasted an hour. The unhappy Spanish nobleman was first overcome, and the German baron succeeded in enveloping him in the sack, took him upon his back, and laid him at the feet of the emperor. This is the origin of the phrase, " *give him the sack*," so common in the literature of courting.

GLASS. The discovery of glass is involved in great doubt and uncertainty. The generally received account is that of the Roman writer Pliny, who relates that some ship- wrecked Phœnician mariners having burnt the kali plant on a seashore while cooking their food, were surprised to observe a transparent substance remaining. This accidental circumstance became known to the people of Sidon, who carried out the hint they had in this way received, and hence the discovery of the art. Window-glass appears to have been made in England in the middle of the fifteenth century, and in 1557 a finer kind was manufactured at Crutched Friars, in London. The first flint-glass was made at Savoy House, in the Strand ; and the first plate-glass was made at Lambeth, in 1673, by Venetian workmen, brought over by the Duke of Buckingham.

GLEEMEN. These were minstrels of the Saxon era. They were not only the poets and historians of the time, but

were also buffoons, story-tellers, and jugglers, all these pro-
fessions being sometimes filled by one man.   Among the
early Saxons they were divided into two classes, distinguished by different names, one signifying merry-makers, and
the other harpers.

GLOVES.   These are supposed to have been introduced by the Persians, and their use was regarded by other
nations as effeminate.   As the habits of the Greeks and
Romans became more refined, they in their turn adopted
the use of these articles of attire   It is believed that gloves
were not used in England until the tenth century, and then
only by the nobility and clergy.   They were not worn by
ladies till the latter end of the thirteenth century.

GOD SAVE THE KING.   Our national anthem,
composed in the time of George I., has always been considered of English origin ; but from the amusing " Memoirs
of Madame de Crequy," it appears to have been almost a
literal translation of the cantique which was always sung by
the demoiselles of St. Cyr when Louis XIV. entered the
chapel of that establishment to hear the morning prayer.
The annexed words are verbatim from Madame de Crequy's
" Memoirs " :—" An anthem—or, rather, a national and
religious hymn—the words by Madame de Brinon, and
music by the celebrated Lully.   The words, which I obtained a long time afterwards, were as follows :—

> ' Grand Dieu, sauvez le Roi !
> Grand Dieu, vengez le Roi !
>   Vive le Roi !
>
> Que, toujours glorieux,
> Louis, victorieux !
> Voie ses ennemis
>   Toujours soumis !

Grand Dieu, sauvez le Roi !
Grand Dieu, vengez la Roi !
Vive la Roi ' ' "

It is said by some to have been translated and adapted to the House of Hanover by Handel, the German composer

GOLDEN NUMBER, originally so called, in consequence of its great utility, was written in letters of gold, as an indication of the esteem in which it was held, and is the key or guide to all the Christian festivals ; showing also the changes of the moon, and thereby how to determine the time of Easter. It commences with one, and ends with nineteen, and after a cycle of nineteen years, it will happen on the same day as when it previously began, with one   Its invention is ascribed to Meton, of Athens, about 432 B.C.

GOLD. The offering of gold, frankincense and myrrh by the eastern magi, to our Saviour, implied that he was of man's nature, and that he would be king. Frankincense and myrrh were used in the embalming of bodies in all eastern countries where the inhabitants preserved their dead from putrefaction; and by presenting these ingredients, it showed their belief that he would die, and that his body would be embalmed. Frankincense is a sweet scented gum ; but myrrh is a gum of greater value, and was usually mixed with aloes, a costly wood, the best of which was then more valuable than gold

GOOD FRIDAY. The day of the crucifixion of the Saviour of the world, used to be called Holy Friday ; the week is now called Passion Week. (See *Buns*)

GOODWIN SANDS. These sands were formed by an

107

inundation of the sea in 1100, and are traditionally supposed to have been part of the domains of Godwin, Earl of Kent, and father of Harold. They are situated opposite the Isle of Thanet, in Kent, and run along the coast between the North and South Forelands for about ten miles.

GOOSE AT MICHAELMAS. It is not true that eating goose at Michaelmas had its origin with Queen Elizabeth. Some think it arose from the great festival of St. Michael, which happened at a time when geese were most plentiful ; and it was a custom for the tenant of an estate to present his landlord with a goose on Michaelmas-day. It is a fact that geese are in much better condition at this season, from their having grazed over the stubble land. There was a vulgar opinion, that if you ate goose on Michaelmas day, you would not want money all the year round.

GORDIAN KNOT. According to ancient history this knot was made in the harness of a chariot by Gordius, king of Phrygia, which knot was so intricate as to baffle every attempt to untie it, or even to find out where it began or ended. The oracle of the day having declared that he who succeeded in solving the complication should be the conqueror of the world, Alexander the Great determined to effect it if possible Aware that if he failed, his followers would be dispirited, he determined to separate it with his sword, and with one blow he cut the knot which was fraught with such interest to the whole world. The expression " cutting the Gordian knot," has consequently been used to signify eluding any difficulty or task by bold or unusual means. The story itself is related in Plutarch's " Life of Alexander."

GOSPEL. This word is of Saxon origin, in which language it implies a good word, good tidings, or good news; the last two are very nearly applicable to the Greek term, *evangelion,* which means good tidings.

GOSSIP. This is the ancient name for the sponsors of a child in baptism. It is derived from Anglo-Saxon *god,* and *syp* a relation. Shakespeare has the "gossip's feast," and the "gossip's bowl." Johnson also defines it "a female tattler," and Dryden has—

> " The common chat of gossips when they meet."

(See *Shrew* and *Gossip's Bridle.*)

GOSSIP'S BRIDLE. The brank, or gossip's bridle, is now in disuse, but a few specimens of this uncomfortable penal instrument are preserved as curiosities, and we wish we could add that the vice which they were designed to punish is as great a rarity. It was made of iron hooping, with a flat piece projecting inwards to lie upon the tongue. It was put upon the head of the offender, padlocked behind, and a string was annexed, by which a man led the wearer through the town. One of these is preserved in the ancient church of Walton-upon-Thames, in Surrey. Tradition tells this bridle to have been presented to the parish about two centuries since, by a person of some consequence at that period, whose name was Chester. Its presentation arose from the singular circumstance of his having lost a valuable estate through the idle stories of an unguarded gossip. The instrument bears this inscription :—

> " Chester presents Walton with a bridle,
> To curb women's tongues that *talk* too idle."

GOVERNMENT. There are three forms of govern-

H   97

ment : monarchical, aristocratical, and democratical. The first, is where the sovereign power is vested in one single person. The second, is when the government is entrusted to, or vested in, the nobility, or a few who are privileged to exercise their power, such as in the original state of Venice, Genoa, etc. A democracy, is where the power is placed in the hands of certain rulers, chosen by the people, such as in the United States. In Britain, these three forms are blended together, and participate in the advantages of each. This is termed a limited monarchy : the sovereign, whether male or female, having only certain privileges granted, and can do nothing further without the consent of both houses of parliament; hence it is said, " the king can do no wrong," which implies that his person is sacred and inviolable; that no law can reach him, and that his ministers are responsible for all acts of the crown.

GRACE AT MEALS. The ancient Greeks considered their table as the altar of friendship, and they would not partake of their meals till they had solemnly offered a portion of them to their gods as the first fruits. The ancient Jews always offered up prayers before meat, and the primitive Christians followed their example, which custom is observed to the present time.

GRAVES (Decorated). It was an ancient practice to plants herbs and flowers about the graves of the dead, in token of their belief in the resurrection. The women in Egypt go weekly to pray and weep at the sepulchres of the dead, and it is their usual custom to throw a sort of herb upon the tombs, which, in Turkey and Asia Minor, have cypress planted at the head and feet, and are also adorned with palm-leaves and boughs of myrtle. Between some of the tombs is placed an ornamental chest of stone filled with earth, in which are planted herbs and aromatic flowers, which are regularly cultivated by the females of the family. At Aleppo, they grow myrtles about the graves, because they continue green a long period.

GRAZE THE SKIN. Grass-earth, the grazing or turning up the earth with a plough, whence the customary service of the inferior tenants of the manor of Amersham, Buckinghamshire, to bring their ploughs and do one day's work for their lord, was called *grass-earth* or *grass-hurt;* and we still say the skin is grazed, or slightly hurt; and a bullet *grazes* any place when it gently turns up the surface of what it strikes upon.

GREAT BRITAIN. Britain was the name given to England, Scotland, and Wales united. It was previously called Albion, from the whiteness of its rocks towards the Continent, or the coast of France; or, as some authors think, from the word *Olbion,* which means rich or happy, in regard to its situation and fertility. It was subsequently named Britain, from *pryd* and *cain,* two words implying beauty and white. (See *Albion.*)

GUTTA PERCHA. This substance is the hardened juice of a tree growing in Singapore, Borneo, and other islands of the Eastern Archipelago. In order to procure it, the largest trees are felled, the bark is stripped off, and a milky fluid which exudes from the lacerated surface is collected and poured into a trough, formed by the hollow stem of the plantain leaf On exposure to the air, the liquid quickly coagulates. The first specimen of gutta percha seen in England was sent to the Society of Arts, in 1843, by Dr. Montgomerie. The word "gutta" means a gum which exudes from a tree, and "percha" is derived from "pertscha," the Malayan name for the tree which principally yields the gum.

H.

HABEAS CORPUS. This is a law term, signifying, "You may have the body." This is the great writ of English liberty. It lies where a person, being indicted and imprisoned, has offered sufficient bail, which has been refused, though the case be bailable ; in this case he may have a *habeas corpus* out of the Queen's Bench, in order to remove himself thither, and to answer the cause at the bar of that court.

HABERDASHER. This word is said to be from the German *habt ihr dass*—have you this—the expression of a shopkeeper offering his wares for sale. Others derive it from *berdash*, a name formerly used in England for a certain kind of neck-dress ; and hence a person who made or sold such neck-cloths was called a *berdasher*, or *haberdasher*. Some also derive this from *avoir d'acheter*.

HAIR POWDER. The custom of wearing hair powder, it is said, took its rise from some of the ballad singers in Bartholomew fair, who whitened their heads to make themselves more ridiculous, and to attract the attention of the bystanders. In November, 1746, one hundred barbers were convicted before the commissioners of assize, and fined £20 each, for having in their custody hair powder not made of starch, contrary to Act of Parliament. Its use in ancient times by ladies is shown by Lucian's description of a lady's

100

toilet :—"Slaves bearing silver basins, richly chased ewers, polished mirrors, boxes of cosmetics, are in attendance, dyeing the eyebrows, clipping the nails, fixing false gums, sprinkling, perfuming, curling, twisting, and *powdering the hair.* Some ladies," he says, "take a fancy to convert their natural black tresses into white or yellow, inclining to flame colour, and to this end besmear them all over with pomatum, and then expose them to the scorching rays of the noon-tide sun, sprinkling them with gold-dust or yellow powder."

HALLELUJAH. This expression is frequently used in Jewish hymns ; and from the Jewish they came into the Christian Church. The meaning is, " Praise the Lord."

HALCYON DAYS. According to heathen mythology, Halcyon was the daughter of Æolus (king of storms and winds), and was changed into a kingfisher , but halcyon days are seven days previous and seven days after the winter solstice, as the halcyon laid her eggs at this season, and the weather was unusually calm, from which the ancients considered that she had power over the winds and waves, and that she laid her eggs on the surface of the sea. Dryden thus alludes to the notion,—

> " Amidst our arms as quiet you shall be,
> As halcyons brooding on a winter's sea. "

HALF HOLIDAYS. In many countries, among other curious customs, it was usual to keep holy the afternoon on Saturdays, in order to usher in the Sabbath by religious meditation. People attended vespers in the evening, and whoever neglected to do so was liable to punishment. In Rome, the 26th March is termed Holy Saturday. On the reading of a particular passage in the service in the Sistine chapel, which takes place about half-past eleven, the bells of St. Peter's are rung, the guns of St. Angelo are fired, and all the bells in the city immediately break forth, as if rejoicing in their renewed liberty of ringing. Among the inhabitants of the Sandwich Islands, it was usual to send out a herald to give intelligence of the approach of the Sabbath, and to command its observance ; and the peasants in most Christian countries refused to do any work after the noon of Saturday till the following Monday.

HALOS. These are circles somewhat similar to the rainbow, which appear about the sun and moon, and are sometimes variously coloured. They never appear in a rainy sky, but in a foggy and frosty one ; and are formed by the refraction of the rays of light, without any reflection, as in the rainbow.

HANDS (Shaking), is not exactly known, but is generally supposed, to be of heathen origin, viz. from Fides, the goddess of faith and oaths. Her symbol was a white dog, being the most faithful animal, and a figure where two women are joining hands, as a token of friendship and fidelity. Others are inclined to think that it took its rise from the kissing of hands, which custom originated with the Greeks, and persons were considered atheists who would not kiss their hands on entering the temple. This custom declined with paganism, and shaking hands as a greeting was substituted. The ancient Romans used to give their hands to be kissed by their inferiors; but with their equals they joined hands and embraced. The custom of both kissing and shaking hands is now practised in every country, but the former is becoming obsolete, except as a mark of duty and obedience from the subject to the sovereign.

102

HANGMAN'S WAGES. This is said to be thirteen-pence halfpenny, in allusion to the Halifax law, or the customary law of the Forest of Hardwick, by which every felon taken within the liberty or precincts of the said forest, with goods to the value of the above sum, should, three market days in the town of Halifax, after his apprehension and condemnation, be taken to a gibbet there, and have his head cut off from his body. Dr. Pegge says the office of hangman was, in some parts of the kingdom, annexed to other posts; for the porter of the city of Canterbury was the executioner for the county of Kent in the reign of Henry II. and III., for which he had an allowance from the sheriff, who was reimbursed from the exchequer, of 20s. per annum. As to the fee itself, " thirteen-pence halfpenny," it appears to have been of Scotch extraction. The Scottish mark was a silver coin, in value thirteen-pence halfpenny and two placks, or two-thirds of a penny. There is, however, very good reason to conclude, from the singularity of the sum, that the odious title, " hangman's wages," became at this time (James I.), or soon after, applicable to the sum last named.

HARMONY (Birds of). This is a small greenish bird found in New Zealand, whose notes are so varied and melodious, that a listener might suppose himself surrounded by a hundred singing birds at once. In Van Diemen's Land there is a bird of this kind, whose note resembles the tinkling of a bell, another that appears to have the faculty of laughter.

HATCHMENTS. When a bachelor dies, his arms are painted single or quartered, but never impaled; the ground of the hatchment under the shield is all black. When a maiden dies, her arms alone must be placed in a lozenge,

103

single or quartered, with the ground under the escutcheon all black. When a married man dies, his arms are impaled with his wife's, the ground of the hatchment under his side of the shield is black, his wife's is white; the black side signifies the husband to be dead, and the white side that the wife is living. When a married woman dies, her arms are impaled with her husband's (but no crest), the ground of the hatchment under her side of the shield is black, that of the husband white, to denote that he is living. When a widower dies, his arms are impaled with those of his deceased wife, with his crest, the ground of the hatchment to be all black; the same in the case of a widow, with the exception of the crest. When the man or woman is the last of the family, the death's-head supplies the place of a crest. This is to signify that death has conquered all. Hatchment is derived from achievement, a coat-armour usually affixed to the front of a house.

HEAD (Uncovering the). This is of very ancient origin, as appears from the Grecian and Roman histories. Taking off the hat cannot be a very old practice, as hats have not been worn above two centuries; but probably this custom, like many others, came on by degrees, and as it is a very easy thing to move the hat and put it on again, it might have been adopted on this account. Ladies have a more easy way of showing their respect to their superiors, namely, by a graceful inclination of the head, and bending the knee at the same time. A very curious paragraph on this subject appeared in one of the magazines a month or two back, to the effect that the object of uncovering the head was to show that the person uncovered was a servant by the condition of his hair,—slaves, etc., being close cut. (See *Bonnets.*)

HEALTH (Drinking). This custom existed so long ago as 1134 before the Christian era. Some persons suppose that it arose from Rowena, the daughter of Hengist, drinking to the health of Prince Vortigern in a golden goblet, at an entertainment, in conformity with the Scripture compliment, "O king, live for ever." Others think that when the Danes held tyrannic sway in England, and assassinations were prevalent, a person was afraid to drink in company without a friend saying, "I pledge you," intimating that he pledged himself for his safety whilst drinking. The Romans used to drink as many glasses to the health of their favourite ladies, as there were letters in her name. (See *Wassail, Was Hæl.*)

HEP, HEP, HURRA. In the time of the Crusades, the people of Europe were excited to arms by the inflammatory preaching of one Peter, a hermit, who was in the habit of unfurling a banner with the letters H. E. P. emblazoned on it. These were the initials of the Latin words "*Hierosolyma est perdita,*" which means "Jerusalem is destroyed." Some people whom he addressed, and who were unacquainted with Latin, read these letters as a word, and called it "Hep." Whenever Peter's followers met with an unfortunate Jew, they raised the cry, "Hep, hep, hep, hurra," to hunt him down, and wreak their vengeance on the poor defenceless Israelite, before they encountered the Saracens, who were masters in the Holy Land.

HEPTARCHY (Saxon). The heptarchy included·— first, the kingdom of Kent; founded by Hengist. Second, Sussex, including Surrey; founded by Ella. Third, Wessex, containing part of Cornwall, Devonshire, Dorsetshire, Somersetshire, Wiltshire, Hampshire, and Berkshire;

105

founded by Cerdic. Fourth, Essex, with Middlesex, and part of Hertfordshire, founded by Erchenwin. Fifth, Northumberland, comprising Westmoreland, Cumberland, Northumberland, and a part of Scotland; founded by Ida. Sixth, East Angles, containing Norfolk, Suffolk, and Cambridgeshire; founded by Offa. Seventh, Mercia, taking in the counties of Gloucester, Hereford, Worcester, Warwick, Leicester, Rutland, Northampton, Lincoln, Huntingdon, Bedford, Buckingham, Oxford, Stafford, Derby, Shropshire, Nottingham, and Cheshire; founded by Cridda.

HE'S A BRICK. The phrase, " He's a brick," seems to be of classic origin, as follows :—King Agesilaus being asked by an ambassador from Epirus, why they had no walls for Sparta, replied, " We have." Pointing to his marshalled army, " There, sir, are the walls of Sparta, and every man you see is a brick " Others assign the following origin to the phrase ·—At a duel which took place in Scotland not many years ago, a person who was charged with its preliminary arrangements, carried with him to the ground two bricks, which he so placed as to mark the distance between the combatants when their pistols should be discharged Several shots having taken place without effect, the parties became reconciled, and returned to Glasgow in friendship together One of the seconds being asked how his principal had behaved, answered, " Like a regular brick ;" meaning that he had been as immovable as that which was at his feet at the time when the shots were exchanged. " A brick, both sides alike," means you are the same inside as out; that is, you say and do as you feel, and are the same behind a person's back as before his face.

106

HIGHLAND CLANS. The following is a list of the clans of Scotland, with a description of the particular badge of distinction anciently worn by each clan respectively, and which served as a distinguishing mark of their chiefs :— Buchanan, birch; Cameron, oak; Campbell, myrtle; Chisholm, alder; Colquhoun, hazel; Cumming, common sallow; Drummond, holly; Farquharson, purple foxglove; Ferguson, poplar; Forbes, broom; Frazer, yew; Gordon, joy; Graham, laurel; Grant, cranberry heath, Gunn, rosewood; Lamont, crab-apple-tree; Macalister, five-leaved heath; Mac Donald, bell-heath; M'Donnell, mountain heath; M'Farlane, cypress, M'Dougal, cloudberry bush; Macgregor, pine, M'Intosh, boxwood; Mackay, bulrush; M'Kensie, deer-grass; M'Kinnon, St John's wort; M'Lachlan, mountain ash; M'Lean, blackburg heath; M'Leod, red whortleberries; M'Nab, rose blackberries; M'Neil, sea-grass; M'Pherson, variegated boxwood; M'Quarrie, blackthorn; M'Rea, fir club-moss; Munro, eagle's feathers; Menzies, ash; Murray, juniper; Ogilvy, hawthorn; Oliphant, the great maple; Robertson, fern or branchius; Rose, brier rose; Ross, bear-berries; Sinclair, clover; Stewart, thistle; Sunderland, cat's-tail grass. The chief of each clan was accustomed to wear two eagle's feathers in his bonnet, in addition to the foregoing badge of his clan.

HOAX. This word is now very common in our language. In Richard Head's " Art of Wheedling," published 1434, it is thus used. The mercer cries, " Was ever a man so hocus'd ?" So that " hoax," or, as it was originally written, " hocus," is any species of dexterous imposition, similar to the tricks of the juggler, whose art was termed, " hocus-pocus,"—similar to the modern " presto fly,"—which

107

is generally admitted to be a corruption of *hoc est corpus,* words used in the Roman Catholic mass. The reason this expression applied to sleight of hand tricks was, because at the words, *Hoc est corpus meum,* the priest was supposed to change the bread into the veritable body, etc., and which was in derision termed a species of jugglery.

HOBSON'S CHOICE. This familiar saying, meaning "that or none," is said to have arisen in the following manner :—Hobson was a noted carrier in Cambridge in the time of James I , and it was his custom, in letting out horses, to compel his customer to take that nearest to the stable-door, or none at all. Hobson raised himself to a considerable estate, and did much good in the town, relieving the poor, building a public conduit in the market-place, etc.

HOCKTIDE SPORTS. Ethelred, in 1002, formed the horrible plot of murdering all the Danes in the kingdom ; and in the city of Winchester the massacre commenced ; such as were not actually put to death being mutilated and rendered incapable of any military service. In commemoration of this barbarous stratagem, the " Hocktide Sports," so called from cutting the hamstrings of the victims, were instituted by that king, and have continued, with a short interruption, until of late years. Hocktide is said to be derived from the German *hoch*, high, or from *hogh tijd,* (Dutch) a high time. It is an annual festival to celebrate the final extinction of the Danish power by the death of Hardicanute, 1042. Hock Monday was the second Monday after Easter week. Hock-tide is still observed in Suffolk, Cambridge, and the neighbouring counties, under the corrupted names of *hawkey*, *hockey*, or *horkey*. It was also the day of St. Blazius, also called " blaze-day."

HONEYMOON. This is a common expression, and had its origin with the Saxons, who, before they came to England, had adopted the phrase from a custom among the northern nations, of drinking a beverage which they were extremely fond of, and made principally from honey, for thirty days after a marriage ; and it is stated that Attila, King of Hungary, drank so freely of this liquor on the night of his wedding, that he was found suffocated in bed.

HOOK OR BY CROOK. The destruction caused by the fire of London, in 1666, during which 12,200 houses, etc., were burned down, in very many cases obliterated all the boundary marks requisite to determine the extent of land, and even the very site occupied by buildings previously to this terrible visitation. When the rubbish was removed and the land cleared, the disputes and entangled claims of those whose houses had been destroyed, both as to the position and extent of their property, promised not only interminable occupation to the courts of law, but made inevitable the far more serious evil of delaying the rebuilding of the city until these disputes were settled. Under the necessity of coming to a more speedy settlement of these claims, two of the most experienced land surveyors of that day, a Mr. Hook and Mr. Crook, were appointed to determine the rights of the various claimants, who by the justice of their decision gave general satisfaction. Hence arose the saying above quoted, usually applied to the extrication of persons or things from a difficulty.

HORSE SHOES. Some historians assert that the practice of shoeing horses was introduced into England by William the Conqueror, who instituted an office for the inspection of the farriers, and gave the city of Northampton as a

109

fief to the person who held that office.   Henry de Ferrers, ancestor of the Earl of Derby, and whose descendants still bear in their arms six horse-shoes, received his title (1343 or 1388), probably, from having been inspector, the horses evidently being shod with *iron* (in French *fer*).   The custom of covering the feet of their horses was known to the ancient Greeks and Romans.   Post horses were shod sometimes in the ninth century, but few of any other description ; and we may state that horse-shoes have been found in the graves of some of the old Germans and Vandals in the northern counties, but the antiquity of them cannot be ascertained. Aubrey observes that in his time " It is a thing very common to nail horse-shoes on the thresholds of doors, as it is a common superstition that a witch cannot enter a door thus protected.

HOW A "HOUSE" IS "MADE."   While the Speaker is bowing out the chaplain, the clerk removes the two folio Prayer-Books, and places them in the drawer. Members who are present have the privilege of securing any particular seat for the night.   On the table there are cards with the words, " At prayers," printed, under which the member writes his name ; and having done this, he attaches the card to the back of the seat which he wishes to occupy.   It will readily be supposed that the attendance at prayers will rise and fall according to the demand which may spring up for particular seats.   Prayers being over, the doors are thrown open, and the public admitted.   The Speaker, however, continues to sit at the clerk's table till such time as forty members are present.   A triangular hat lies on the table before him ; he takes it up, and using it in the same way as chairmen of public meetings use their forefinger when counting "hands," counts aloud those members who have been present at prayers, beginning with the Ministerial side (the right-hand side), and taking any who may be in the gallery first.   In the meantime members are dropping in, and the Sergeant-at-Arms and the other officers direct them towards the Opposition side of the house, that the Speaker may not be puzzled in his counting.   If members fall short of the quorum, the Speaker waits patiently for more to come in ; but if forty do not present themselves before the hand of the clock points to four, he rises and says, " The house is adjourned."   If he arrives successfully at thirty-nine, he immediately pronounces " forty," himself counting for the fortieth, and proceeds to take possession of his proper chair or throne, and the house is said to be " made."

HOW DO YOU DO ?   This phrase is principally confined to the English, and is a very absurd question when taken literally , as it implies, How does your business answer ? or, What are you busy about? and may be answered,—I am doing well ; or, I am busy writing,—instead of telling how your health is.   The French say, How do you carry yourself ? Italians, How do you stand ?   Germans, How goes it ? How do you find yourself ?   The Dutch say, How do you sail ?   This arose from their being originally fishermen or sailors, and instead of—Good morning, they say, May you eat a good dinner !   The Chinese salutation is—Have you eaten your rice ? which is a proper expression in a country where the poorer classes are in a state of starvation.   In some parts of Egypt they say—How do you sweat ?   This also is a proper question where the climate is very hot, and where profuse perspiration is the great promoter of health.

HOWL (Funeral). The Irish, in the present day, make a great outcry on the decease of their friends, hoping thus to awaken the soul, which they suppose might otherwise be inactive. It was known to the Greeks and Romans ; the latter had their *præficæ*, whose duty it was to superintend the manner and form of their lamentations ; and it is practised now in Albania and all over the East.

HUMAN RACE. The human race has been divided into five different classes : Caucasian, Mongolian, Ethiopian, Malayan, and American. The Caucasian race includes the Europeans, with the exception of the Lapps and Finns. The Mongolian race includes the Lapps and Finns, all the Asiatics north and east of the Caspian Sea, the Chinese, Japanese, and Esquimaux. The Ethiopian race includes Negroes, Hottentots, Kaffirs. The Malayan includes the inhabitants of the Malay peninsula, and native inhabitants of Australia, Van Diemen's Land, New Guinea, etc. The native American races are distinct. Some writers, however, make only three divisions—namely, Caucasian, Mongolian, and Ethiopian ; under this arrangement the Malay and Indian races are identified with the Mongols. The white and brownish nations of Europe, West Asia, and Northern Africa, are considered the most handsome on the globe. The yellow, or olive-coloured, which includes Chinese, Mongols, and Calmucs, are next. The jet black Negroes, and other Africans of various shades follow, and have woolly hair, thick lips, flat noses, and downy skins. And the Australians on the Continent, and in the Indian and Pacific Oceans, are dark brown, and the least favoured of all.

HUE AND CRY. This is the old common law process of pursuing "with horn and with voice," from hundred to hundred, and county to county, all robbers and felons. Formerly the *hundred* was bound to make good all loss occasioned by the robberies therein committed, unless the felons were taken; but by subsequent laws it is made answerable only for damage committed by riotous assemblies. The pursuit of a felon was aided by a description of him in the *Hue and Cry*, a gazette established for advertising felons, in 1710.

HUMBUG. There are various stories as to the derivation of this word, one of the best authenticated of which states that it is a corruption of Hamburg, and originated in the following manner :—During a period when war prevailed on the Continent, so many false reports and lying bulletins were fabricated at Hamburg, that at length, when any one wished to signify his disbelief of a statement, he would say, " That's from Hamburg," or " That's a Hamburg ;" or he would simply sneer, " Hamburg !" which finally got corrupted into " humbug."

HUSBAND. This word is Anglo-Saxon, and signifies the bond of the house, or family housebond ; as by him the family is formed, united, and bound together, which, on his death, is disunited and scattered. Hence we account for farmers and petty landowners being called, so early as the twelfth century, *husbandi*, as appears in a statute of David II., king of Scotland. This etymology of the word appears plainer in the orthography of the thirteenth and fourteenth centuries, in which the word is often found written, housebond.

HYMNS. These were components in the religious ceremonies of the Egyptians, Assyrians, Greeks, Romans, and other ancient nations; and the mention in the Bible of " Jubal's lyre," " David's harp," " Miriam's song," etc , shows how largely music was employed in early times and in the Jewish ceremonies. The hymns of the early Christians, adverted to by St. Paul and St. James, were probably a species of carols. (See *Carols.*)

I.

IGNIS FATUUS. This is the Latin name for what is called Jack-o'-lantern, or Will-o'-the-wisp. Literally, it means the foolish fire. It is produced by the phosphorus evolved from decayed leaves and other vegetable and animal matter in a state of decomposition.

INDEPENDENTS. These are so called from maintaining that all Christian congregations are so many "independent" religious societies. The first Independent Church in England was established by Mr. Jacob, in the year 1616. A sect of Scottish, or new Independents, also sprang up in that country in 1797.

INDEX EXPURGATORIUS. This is a catalogue of the works forbidden by the Church of Rome to be read by the laity, on account of their containing heresy. The first *Index Expurgatorius,* or *Index Librorum Prohibitorum,* as it is sometimes called, was made public at Louvain in 1546.

INFANTRY. One of the monarchs of Spain being defeated by the Moors, his daughter assembled a body of foot soldiers, followed the enemy, and totally overthrew them. In honour of this event they received the title of infantry, as the Spanish princesses are called *infantas*

114

INFERNAL MACHINE. The following account of an infernal machine, in 1587, is given by an old French writer. In the reign of Henry III., M. Malabre invented an infernal machine, and caused it to be conveyed to the Seigneur de Millan d'Allegre. It was a box containing thirty-six pistol barrels, each of them loaded with a couple of bullets. This box was so contrived that, on opening it, each of these barrels was to discharge its contents at the same moment, firing off seventy-two balls. It was sent with a forged letter, as from his sister, signifying that she desired his acceptance of a curiosity, which the bearer would instruct him how to open. This bearer was the inventor's servant, who had been taught the manner of opening the box, but was a stranger to what it contained. Accordingly it was opened by his direction and in the presence of M. Millan d'Allegre, when the pistols were all discharged, but the gentleman and the servant were only slightly wounded. The inventor was instantly apprehended, and executed in the latter end of September, 1587.

ILLUSTRIOUS. The Emperor Constantine was the first who received the title of Illustrious. This title was more particularly given to those princes who had distinguished themselves in battle ; but it was not made hereditary. The ancient lawyers of Italy were not content with calling their kings *illustres*, for they went a grade higher, and styled them *super illustres*.

INNOCENTS' DAY. This day (December 28), also named Childermas-day, was deemed of especial ill omen ; the superstitious never married on it, and the coronation of Edward IV. was put off till the Monday, because the preceding Sunday was Childermas-day. Children were flogged or whipped by their parents, in bed, on the morning of this festival, in order that the memory of Herod's massacre of the innocents might be remembered more strongly; and processions of children walked through the streets, and recited verses in commemoration of the event.

INVENTION OF THE CROSS. The Romish Church celebrates this day (31d May) as a festival to commemorate the invention or finding of a wooden cross, supposed to be the tiue one, by Helena, the mother of Constantine the Great.

J.

JACOBITE. This word is derived from Jacobus, and was a sort of reproachful epithet applied to those who disapproved of the revolution of King William, and supported the interest of James. It is also applied to those who vindicate the rights of passive obedience, and the Divine right of kings; in which sense it has the same signification as the woid Tory. (See *Whig.*)

JEHOVAH. In Hebrew, *Yehovah* is the Scripture name of the Supreme Being. If, as is supposed, this name is from the Hebrew substantive verb, the word denotes the Permanent Being, as the primary sense of the substantive verb in all languages is, to be fixed, to stand, to remain or abide. This is a name peculiarly appropriate to the eternal Spirit, the unchangeable God, who describes Himself thus: *I am that I am.* The Rabbis say it is compounded of pret. sing. 3 m. היה, the fut. sing. 3 m. ייה, and הלה part. active (see Revelation i. 4 . ὁ ὢν καὶ ὁ ἦν καὶ ὁ ἐρχόμενος.) By the word Jehovah is understood the ineffable name of God, or His Divine essence. It was held so sacred by the Hebrews, that they would never read it when they came to it in any writing, but instead thereof, they pronounced the word "Adonai," which signifies Lord.

JEWISH FESTIVALS. The Jews had, besides those already described, their feasts of New Moon, of Trumpets, of Pentecost, of Dedication, and others, all of which are of a religious character, and were celebrated in order to keep up friendship and unity among the different tribes.

JEWISH SACRIFICES. Burnt offerings may be classed under two heads, the bloody and unbloody, the first of which were divided into three sorts : first, whole burnt-offerings; second, sin or trespass-offerings; third, peace-offerings. A whole burnt-offering was the most excellent, since it was all consecrated to God, the victim being wholly consumed upon the altar; and this was the most ancient, having been offered by Noah, Abraham, and other patri-archs, and the ceremonies were numerous and varied. There were five sorts of animals offered : viz. oxen, sheep, goats, pigeons, and turtle-doves, care being taken to choose those free from blemish. Unbloody offerings, which were termed meat-offerings, consisted of wheat, bread, ears of corn, and parched grain, with libations of wine, mixed with oil and frankincense. There was also a quantity of flour, wine, and oil, presented with every animal that was sacri-ficed, the wine being poured on the brow of the animal, to consecrate it.

JOHN O'GROAT'S HOUSE. Duncan's Head, in Caithness-shire, is the most northerly part of Britain. John O'Groat caused a house to be erected there, which became famous for its situation, and from being built for three

117

brothers, each of whom had an equal share in the house and premises ; but, in process of time, their families multiplied, and there were no less than eight proprietors of the name of Groat, all of whom met at an anniversary dinner, which, for some years, was amicably celebrated ; but afterwards a dispute arose which should first enter the door, and sit at the head of the table, when old John interposed, and built a room of an octagonal shape, with eight doors, and made a table with eight corners At the next anniversary he made each enter by a separate door, and take his seat at one part of the table, which put an end to their domestic squabbles. The traditionary story respecting Malcolm, Gavin, and John de Groat having arrived from Holland and purchased the lands of Duncansbay, and commemorating their arrival by an annual festive meeting, is well known.

JUDGES' CIRCUITS. It is not, perhaps, generally known at how very remote a period the practice of judges going the circuit prevailed ; but on consulting 1 Samuel vii. 16, we find this extraordinary confirmation : "And he (Samuel) went from year to year in circuit to Bethel, and Gilgal, and Mizpeh, and judged Israel in all those places."

JUDGES' COIF. The use of the coif was to cover the *tonsura clericalis*—clerical crown. In the Romish Church, tonsure is the first ceremony used for devoting a person to the service of God and the Church. Spelman conjectures that coifs were introduced to hide the tonsure of such renegade clerks as were still tempted to remain in the secular courts in the quality of advocates, notwithstanding their prohibition by canon law. The modern coif is a badge of a serjeant-at-law, who is called Serjeant of the Coif; it is of lawn, and is worn on the head, under the cap, when they are created, and ever after. In ancient days, coifs were worn by knights, which were iron skull-caps under their helmets.

JULIAN YEAR. In the time of Julius Cæsar, the year was reduced to such disorder, that the winter months had fallen back to the autumn. To restore them to their proper season, he formed a year of 445 days, which has been styled the year of confusion. He afterwards instituted a solar year of 365 days 6 hours, which is now known by the name of the Julian year. In order to adjust this year to the annual revolution of the earth, a day was appointed to be intercalated every fourth year, in the month of February; this day, from its position in the Roman calendar, was called bissextile. The Julian year, however near as it approximated to the truth, was not the truth; the true time of the annual revolution of the sun in the ecliptic is 365 days, five hours, and nearly forty-nine minutes, which falls short by a few minutes of the time assumed by the Julian year. This difference may appear trifling, but in the course of 131 years it amounted to a whole day. To remedy this, Pope Gregory XIII. caused the calendar to undergo another correction. In 1580, he ordered ten days to be cut out of the month of October, so that the fourth was reckoned the fifteenth day; and to prevent such retrocession in future, in addition to the Julian regeneration with respect to the Bissextile year, he ordered that the years 1600, 2000, 2400, and every fourth century in succession, should have an intercalation of a day.

K.

KENT (Holy Maid of). Elizabeth Burton was incited

by the Roman Catholic party to hinder the Reformation by pretending to inspirations from heaven. She foretold that Henry VIII. would die a speedy and violent death, and direful calamities would happen to the nation, if he divorced his wife Catherine of Spain, and married Anne Boleyn. She and her confederates were hanged at Tyburn, April 20, 1534.

KEYS. These are referred to in several parts of Scripture, and Homer, in his Odyssey, describes the key of the storehouse of Ulysses, as of a large curvature. It was in shape like a reaping hook, and made of brass, but the handle was of ivory, though locks and keys in the East are very commonly made of wood.

KILKENNY CATS. The story has been so long current that it has become a proverb,—" as quarrelsome as the Kilkenny cats : " two of the cats in which city are asserted to have fought so long and so furiously that nought was found of them but two tails. The correct version of this saying is this :—During the rebellion which occurred in Ireland in 1798, Kilkenny was garrisoned by a regiment of Hessian soldiers, whose custom it was to tie together in one of their barrack-rooms two cats by their respective tails, and then to throw them face to face across a line generally used for drying clothes. The cats naturally became infuriated, and scratched each other in the abdomen until death ensued to one or both of them. The officers were made acquainted with these barbarous acts of cruelty, and resolved to put an end to them. For this purpose an officer was ordered to inspect each barrack-room daily, and report its state. The soldiers, determined not to lose the daily torture of the cats, generally employed one of their comrades to watch the approach of the officer. On one occasion he neglected his duty, and the officer was heard ascending the stairs while the cats were undergoing their customary torture. One of the troopers seized a sword from the arm-rack, and with a single blow divided the tails of the cats. The cats escaped through the open windows of the room, which was entered instantly afterwards by the officer, who inquired what was the cause of the two bleeding cats' tails being suspended on the line, and was told in reply that " two cats had been fighting in the room ; that it was found impossible to separate them ; and they fought so desperately that they had devoured each other up, with the exception of their two tails."

KING. The origin of this word is derived from the Saxon *cyng*, *cynig*, or *cyning*, signifying " a chief, a leader, one that attracts or draws," and from *can*, "to bear " or "produce," or *ken*, " knowledge," wherewith every king is supposed to be endowed The Latin *rex*, the Scythian *reix*, the Punic *pesch*, the Spanish *rey*, the Gaelic *righ*, and the French *roy* —all these are said to come from the Hebrew *rasch*, the literal meaning of which is the " chief head."

KISSING HANDS. This is not only a very ancient and nearly universal custom, but it has alike been participated by religion and society. From the remotest times men saluted the sun, moon, and stars, by kissing the hand. Solomon says of the flatterers and suppliants of his time, that they ceased not to kiss the hands of their patrons till they had obtained the favours which they had solicited. This custom prevailed in Rome ; but it varied. In the first ages of the republic it seems to have been only practised by

121

inferiors to their superiors ; equals gave their hands and embraced.

KNIGHTHOOD.   In the barbarous ages of ignorance and superstition, some of the nobility, having nothing else to do, used to wander about the country in search of adventures, and devoted themselves to the protection and rescue of ladies (see *Chivalry*), many of whom were forcibly carried away by men that regarded neither justice nor humanity.   These were called knights-*errant*, and of them many marvellous and fabulous stories are told.   The order of the knights of the round table, instituted by Prince Arthur, is the most ancient on record.   In almost every European state there are different orders of knighthood.   We have no account of the order of the Bath till the time of Richard II. who created four knights : they bathed themselves, and used several religious ceremonies the night before their creation ; and up to the reign of Charles II. it was usual for the sovereign to create a certain number of knights of this order prior to his coronation.   Knights Templars were a military order of monks, established at Jerusalem in the twelfth century, for the protection of the temple, sepulchre, etc., abolished in 1312, in consequence of their vicious and tyrannical conduct.   The Temple, London, is so called from having once been a residence of these knights.

KNITTING.   This art is first noticed about the commencement of the sixteenth century ; and, according to some, originated in Scotland, whence it found its way into France.   It is related that in 1564, William Ryder, an apprentice of Master Thomas Burdett, having accidentally seen, in the shop of an Italian merchant, a pair of knit worsted stockings, made a pair exactly like them, which he presented to William Earl of Pembroke, and that these were the first stockings knit in England of woollen yarn.

KNIVES It is difficult to determine the precise date of the introduction of knives; for, doubtless, the necessity for cutting implements suggested at a very early age some kind of knife, however rude its construction. They were very early manufactured in Sheffield.

L.

LABYRINTH. This is a Greek word, probably derived from the Egyptians, and signifying originally a vast edifice, the passages through which were so intricate, that it was extremely difficult to find a way out of them. The four most remarkable for size and magnificence were those of Egypt, Crete, Lemnos, and Etruria; all were intended for tombs, and by their intricacy were supposed to represent the vicissitudes of life, and the wanderings of the soul after death We apply this term to a combination of walks in a park or garden, from which egress is difficult on account of their complication. The ancients used the term in a figurative sense, to signify discussions that return constantly to the point whence they set out, and other similarly confused species of discourse. With us it means a complication of difficult circumstances that greatly embarrass us.

LADY AND THE LAMB. At Kidlington, Oxford, the people had a custom on the Monday after Whitsun week, to run after a live fat lamb. The manner was that the maids of the town, having their hands tied behind them, should pursue the lamb until one caught it with her

123

teeth. Hence the term "The lady and the lamb." The victim was then dressed, and, with the skin hanging on, carried on a pole before the "lady" and her companions to the green. Here a morris-dance was performed, and the rest of the day spent in dancing and merry making. The day following, part of the lamb was roasted, the rest baked and boiled, for the lady's feast, where she presided, with her companions, music, and attendants.

LADY. This word is derived from the Saxon *hlaf-dig, hlæfdiga, hlæfdia,* loaf-giver, or bread-giver. It was formerly a custom for the affluent to reside constantly at their manor-house, and for the mistress of the mansion to distribute a quantity of bread with her own hands; hence she was called *hlæfdia,* since corrupted to *lady.* The term *gentleman,* though now applied to every person of respectability and unimpeachable character, was originally conferred by Richard II., in 1430, on all those whose ancestors were freemen, and owed obedience to their prince only.

LAMMAS. This day (first of August) in the Romish Church, is generally called "St. Peter in the Fetters," in commemoration of this apostle's imprisonment. Some authors say Lammas signifies "lamb" mass; others think it takes its origin from the Saxon *hlammæsse, hlafmæssee,* loaf mass, or bread feast, an offering of thanks made from the first new wheat, about the first of August, in gratitude for an abundant harvest. It was a custom in some places for the tenants to bring wheat to their lord, of the current year's growth, on this day. On Lammas-day free pasturage commenced, and this custom is still continued in many places; and till within these last few years, Battersea Fields (now Park) themselves were Lammas land.

124

LAUREATE (Poet). There are no records which settle the origin of the institution in this kingdom. There was a court poet as early as the reign of Henry III. Chaucer, on his return from abroad, first assumed the title of poet laureate, and in the twelfth year of Richard II. obtained a grant of an annual allowance of wine. James I., in 1615, granted to his laureate a yearly pension of 100 marks ; and in 1630 this stipend was augmented by letters patent of Charles I. to £100 per annum, with an additional grant of one tierce of Canary wine, to be taken out of the king's store yearly.

LEAP-YEAR. The ladies' privilege, which is ordinarily said to be permitted in this year, took its origin in the following manner :—By an ancient Act of the Scottish Parliament, passed in the reign of Margaret, about the year 1228, it was " Ordonit that during ye reign of her maist blessit Majestie, ilka maiden ladee, of baith high and low estait, shall hae liberty to speak ye man she likes ; gif he refuses to take her to be his wif, he shall be mulct in the sum of an hundrity pundis or less, as his estait may be, except and always gif he can make it appear that he is betroth it to anither woman, then he shall be free." Leap-year, consisting of 366 days, is found by dividing the current year by four. If there be no remainder, it is leap-year ; if otherwise, the remainder shows how many years it is after it.

LEAPING THE DITCH. Senilly, in France, was formerly known for a very ancient custom, called the *Saut de Senilly,* which formed part of the feudal rights of the abbey of the parish, but was abolished at the Revolution. A ditch of a certain width and rather deep was dug and

125

filled with water, and all the male inhabitants who had married since the preceding Trinity Sunday were bound to leap over it, or pay a fine of three livres one denier, and eighteen bushels of oats.   On these occasions, the seneschal of the castle, accompanied by his officers, all in grand costume, presided gravely at the fulfilment of this singular custom; the ditch was examined to see that it had the necessary width, and that the water was clean, as required by the charter, after which the recorder of the abbey called the newly married men by name, and these on a signal given took the leap, sometimes landing safely on the other side, and often alighting in the water midway, to the great delight of the spectators.   Those who accomplished the task successfully were presented with a bottle of wine, and had the right to cut a willow on the territory of the abbey to make a cradle.   This practice was last observed in 1788.

LEASE (Under).   A person is said to make an under-lease, or to under-let, when, being a tenant for years, he re-lets his holding for part of the term he has in it, or being a tenant from year to year, he lets again to another tenant.

LEATHER BOTTLES. The people in the East keep their milk, wine, water, and other liquors in leathern bottles, made commonly of goat-skins.   When the animal is killed, they cut off its feet, and its head, and so they draw off its skin, without cutting open the belly.   They afterwards sew up the places where the legs and tail were cut off.   The country people of the East never go a journey without a small leathern bottle of water hanging by their side.   The great bottles are made of the skin of a he-goat, and the small ones of a kid skin.   These bottles,

126

when old, are liable to break and burst. Hence the propriety of not putting new wine in old bottles. (See *Cork.*)

LEEKS (Wearing). It is stated that they are worn by the Welsh in honour of their tutelar saint, St. David, who rendered them great service in their wars against the Saxons, particularly on the 1st of March, 640, when it is asserted that they gained a complete victory over them in a field of leeks ; but, as their dresses very much resembled those of the enemy, each Welshman put a leek in his hat, to distinguish his friend from his foe.

LESSEE. This describes a person to whom a lease is made, and a lessor is one who grants a lease.

LICENSE (Marrying by). This custom is generally supposed to have been introduced with the Reformation, when, in Shrewsbury, no woman could marry without a license from the king, to whom she with her first husband paid the sum of ten shillings. If she took a second husband the sum was doubled.

LINE (Passing the). The ordeal to which novices are subjected on crossing the equator, though the ceremony has been greatly changed, as well as the purpose to which the fines received on account of it are applied, is by no means a practice of modern date, as appears by the following extract from Merolla's " Voyage to Congo," in the year 1682 :—" A sort of court is erected among them, by consent of the commander ; then two judges, dressed accordingly, sit at table, where they take full cognisance of all such as have not yet passed the line ; and then, as if it were a great crime, they mulct them according to their quality. Such as are not ready to pay their fines, or at

127

least willing to offer something, are seized in a trice, and by a rope round their middles hauled up to the main-yard arm, whence they are let thrice successively into the sea. From this punishment or a fine none are exempt, and, it is said, with the latter they *maintain a church.*"

LITTLE STROKES FELL GREAT OAKS. Pliny reports that there are to be found flints worn by the feet of pismires, which is not altogether unlikely, for the ants have their roads or footpaths so worn by travelling that they may be easily observed.

LIVERIES. The custom of clothing servants in liveries originated with our British ancestors, who clothed their vassals in all sorts of uniform, in order to distinguish families of distinction, in the same manner as they painted arms and symbols on their clothes and armour.

LLOYD'S. This is frequently named in connection with shipping affairs. Mr. Lloyd kept a coffee-house in Cornhill, where shipping agents and insurance brokers met to transact business. Subsequently his name was applied to a set of rooms in the Royal Exchange, kept up by subscription for the same purpose. *Lloyd's List,* is a publication in which the news received in the rooms is published.

LOAF SUGAR. The art of refining sugar appears to have been known at least as early as the reign of Henry VIII., as a roll of provisions of that period mentions " two loaves of sugar, weighing 16 lb. 2 oz., at — per pound." A letter from Sir Edward Wotton to Lord Cobham, dated Calais, March 6th, 1546, informs him that he had taken up

128

for his lordship twenty-five sugar loaves, at six shillings a loaf, " whiche is eighte pence a pounde." (See *Sugar.*)

LOG BOOK Coelbren y Beirrd, or the wooden memorial of the Bards. was used by them as a kind of almanac, or wooden memorandum book, on which they noted such things as they wished to preserve from oblivion. The Staffordshire clog, or log. is the same as the wooden almanac used among the ancient Britons. From this originated the " log book " now universally kept on board ship, and so termed from the book being copied from the log-board used in navigation, etc. There is an instrument similar to it, called a tally, or a piece of wood cut with notches, in two corresponding parts, of which one was kept by the debtor, and one by the creditor; this was formerly the way of keeping accounts. Hence came the Tally Office, and tellers (of the Exchequer). In 1834 a great accumulation of tallies were housed at Westminster, and an order went forth that they were to be privately and confidentially burned in a stove in the House of Lords. The stove, overgorged with these sticks, set fire to the panelling. the panelling to the House of Lords, the latter to the House of Commons, and the two houses were reduced to ashes The word tally is supposed to be derived from the Welsh word *talu*, to pay, or from the French word *taille.*

LOINS (Gird up your). The ancient Jews and others, wore their garments very long, large, and loose, both for elegance and convenience. The eastern parts of the earth being extremely hot by day, and very cold at night, they usually slept without undressing. The upper garment was at least six yards in length, and five in breadth, which of course must have been very troublesome to the traveller; he was, therefore, obliged to tuck it up, and fold it round him by means of a girdle fastened round the waist or loins. Hence the expression, "Gird up your loins."

LONDON STONE. This is a fragment of puzzling antiquity. It stands in the south wall of St. Swithin's church, Cannon Street, London, and is reduced to a mere shell of worn, worm-eaten stone. Though now hardly noticed, it was once regarded with reverence, from a strange superstition that the fate of the city depended upon it— that the fortunes of London depended upon its preservation, as Troy on its Palladium, or the destinies of Scotland on the misshapen mass of granite let into the coronation chair at Westminster Abbey. Since Camden's time, antiquaries have pronounced this stone a Roman military station, from which the Romans began the measurement of their military ways, as from a centre.

LORD CHANCELLOR. This office was known to the courts of the Roman emperors, where it originally seems to have signified a chief scribe or secretary, who was afterwards invested with several judicial powers, and a general superintendence of the rest of the officers of the prince. Under the Emperor Carinus, one of his door-keepers, with whom he entrusted the government of the city, was denominated *Cancellarius;* and from this humble origin, the appellation has, by a singular fortune, risen into the title of the first great office in the state.

LORD LIEUTENANT. The lord lieutenant of a county is a nobleman selected by the sovereign from among the principal peers of the kingdom; and formerly

130

his power was much more extensive than at present. His business is to form, arm, and array local armies, troops, regiments, etc., the men of which are termed "militia," now deemed almost unnecessary, on account of the regular standing army, regiments of yeomanry cavalry, and volunteers, the officers of which are frequently men of fortune. Through the efficiency of the latter bodies, in cases of emergency, our standing army can at any time be sent abroad, and yet leave the country in a proper state of defence.

LOTTERIES. The earliest lottery on record took place in the year 1569; it consisted of 40,000 lots, at 10s. each lot. The prizes were silver plate, and the profits arising from it were applied to repair the havens of the kingdom. It was drawn at the west door of St. Paul's Cathedral, and the drawing, which began January 11th, continued incessantly day and night till May 6th, in the same year. There were then only two lottery offices in London.

LOVE TOKENS The ancient English custom of giving these tokens on the 20th of August, was a very wise and far-seeing plan for settling young ladies in life by marriage. It was the custom in England, years since, for " enamoured maydes and gentilwomen" to give to their favourite swains, as tokens of their love, little handkerchiefs about three or four inches square, wrought round about, often in embroidery, with a button or tassel at each corner, and a small one in the centre. The finest of these favours were edged with narrow gold lace or twist; and then, being folded up in four cross folds, so that the middle might be seen, they were worn by the accepted lovers in their hats or on their breasts.

These favours became at last so much in vogue that they were sold ready-made in the shops, in Queen Elizabeth's time, from sixpence to sixteen-pence a piece.

LOW SUNDAY. This is the first Sunday after Easter. It is likewise styled Quasimodo Sunday, from the commencement of the hymn for mass on that day; and as the ceremonies and services were of a lower degree, and less pompous than at Easter, it received the title of Low Sunday.

LULLABY. This means a song to quiet infants, and took its rise in superstition, from a supposed fairy called Elaby Gathon, whom nurses invited to watch over sleeping babes, that they might not be changed for others. From this supposititious practice arose the term changeling, or infant changed.

M.

MAC. This term implies son, and is used by the Scotch before surnames, as Mac Donald, Mac Arthy, etc., or son of Donald, son of Arthy, etc. The Irish prefix O before names, as O'Connell, O'Brien, etc., which means a grandson. The Welsh use Ap, as Ap Rice, Ap Maurice, Ap Howell, etc., which means son of Rice, son of Maurice, son of Howell, hence the names Powell, Price, etc. But the English adopt various devices with their names; for instance, adding a letter or syllable, thus, Will, or William, will make Wills, Wilson, Willet, Williams, Williamson, etc., Robert, Roberts, Robertson, Robins, Robbins, Robson, Robinson, etc. (See *Surnames.*)

MAGNA CHARTA. This was signed by King John

and the barons of England at Runnymead, a meadow on the banks of the Thames, between Staines and Windsor ; 15th June, 1215. It provides that fines or amercements shall never destroy a man, and therefore all such as are beyond a man's means are unlawful. It saves a freeholder's estate, a merchant's merchandise, a scholar's books, a workman's tools, etc., and also by it 10*d.* was fixed as the price per day of a cart with two horses, and 1*s.* 2*d.* with three.

MAIDS (Biddenden). A distribution of bread and cheese takes place at Biddenden, Kent, on Easter Sundays, the expense being defrayed from the rental of twenty acres of land, the reputed bequest of the Biddenden maids, two sisters, named Chalkhurst, who, tradition states, were born joined together by the hips and shoulders, in 1100 ; and having lived in that state to the age of 34, died within six hours of each other. Cakes bearing a corresponding impression of the figures of two females, are given on Easter-day to all who ask for them. This legend has been deemed fabulous, and it is said that the print on the cakes is of modern origin, and also, that the land was given by two maiden ladies, named Preston.

MAJESTY. Henry VIII. was the first who took the title of Majesty, which is still retained by his successors. Before his reign, the sovereigns were generally addressed as "My Liege," or "Your Grace," the latter of which was conferred on Henry IV. "Excellent Grace" was given to Henry VI. "Most high and mighty Prince," to Edward IV. "Highness," and sometimes "Grace," to Henry VII. ; this Henry VIII. also took, but it gave way to the more honourable or lofty expression, "Majesty," by which

133

title he was addressed by Francis I. Pope Leo conferred the title of " Defender of the Faith," on Henry VIII. as a compliment to his defence against Martin Luther. James I. added the epithet " Sacred," or " Most excellent majesty." Titles are merely appellations of dignity or honour. The monarch of England is styled the King (or Queen) of Great Britain, Ireland, etc. The title of His Most Christian Majesty was conferred by the pope on Louis XI., but since the Revolution of 1789 it has been in disuse. Louis Philippe was King of the French ; Napoleon III. is styled Emperor, and sometimes the title of Most Christian Majesty is now applied. The monarch of Spain has many titles, the principal is Most Catholic Majesty. The Pope has the title of Holiness, and Emperors have that of Imperial Majesty. The title of Emperor has pre-eminence above that of kings or other sovereigns. The sovereign of Turkey is called Grand Seignior, Sultan, and Highness. There are other titles in different parts, such as that of Doge,the chief magistrate of Venice and Genoa. The sovereign of Algiers is called the Dey. Bey also denotes a superior governor of the Turkish empire. Viceroy is the superior governor of a kingdom, in the name, and instead of, the king or queen, as the Viceroy of Ireland.

MAN. It was ordained by the great Creator of the world, that man should rule over every other creature, for which purpose he was' endowed with faculties which no other class of beings possesses. Man walks erect, can laugh, speak, sing, reason ; and enjoys numerous other powers which are not inherent in any other animal.

MANGANESE. This is a brilliant metal, of a darkish white colour, inclining to grey, very brittle, of considerable

134

hardness, and not easily fusible. It is found in great abundance in most parts of Europe, particularly in Sweden and Germany ; large quantities are now dug in Devonshire, Cornwall, and Ireland. It is used by glass manufacturers to remove the greenish hue seen in white glass ; and by the bleachers of fustian and muslin.

MANNA is a gum which flows from a species of the ash tree in the southern parts of Europe.

MARRIAGE. The regard paid to marriage in different nations is singularly illustrative of various degrees of progress. Many savages have not arrived at the idea of marriage, and their wives are essentially a part of their property. In some cases the tie is of such a nature that it affords not even a presumption as to parentage ; and they recognise kinship only on the mother's side. This is the case with the South Sea Islanders generally. It was so with the ancient Celts, Greeks, Cossack hordes, etc. By tracing up the idea of marriage, we can account for the notion which we find in every part of the world, that a man is regarded as no relation to his own children. Only as things improved and the probability of parentages became greater, kinship through females only was abandoned. Among the early Jews, Abraham married his half-sister, Nahor his brother's daughter, and Amram his father's sister. These women were not then regarded as relatives. At a later period they would have been so. Even among ourselves, a man is no relation to his own children, except born in wedlock. In every step, from the treatment of women as chattels to the sacred idea of matrimony, we find clear evidence that the change has been one of progress, and not of degradation. Many nations have traditions of

135

the origin of marriage. The Egyptians attributed it to Menes, the Greeks to Cecrops, and the Hindus to Soctaketer.

MARRIAGE (Morganatic). In this the left hand is given instead of the right, and the marriage is generally contracted between a man of superior and a woman of inferior rank, in which it is stipulated that the latter and her children shall not enjoy the rank, or inherit the possessions, of the former. The children are legitimate. These marriages are frequently contracted in Germany by royalty and the higher nobility. Our George I. was thus married ; and later, the King of Denmark to the Countess of Danner, August 7th, 1850.

MARSHAL (Earl) To prevent the confusion of different families assuming the same coat (of arms), was the business of the Earl Marshal, who had the arrangement of the field of battle And hence the Court of Chivalry and the College of Arms to register arms and pedigrees, which last was not incorporated till about the time of Edward IV. The office of Earl Marshal soon became hereditary in the family of Mowbray, from whom it passed by marriage to the Howards, with whom it continues to this day.

MARSHAL (Field). This title was created in this country in the month of January, 1736. It is thus mentioned :—" His majesty (George I.) has been pleased to erect a new post of honour, under the title of Marshal of the armies of Great Britain, and to confer the same on the Duke of Argyle and the Earl of Orkney, as the two eldest generals.

MARTINMAS. This is the 11th November, and the word is derived from Martin and mass. St. Martin was bishop of Tours in the fourth century, and was styled the wise and good man. The Martinalia was an ancient general festival; wines were then tasted, and cleanly racked from the lees, and the vinalia was removed to this day. St. Martin was hence made typical of Bacchus, the god of wine.

MARQUIS. Marchio, or marquis, was first so called from the government of marches and frontier countries. Such were the marches of Wales and Scotland, while each continued to be an enemy's country. In Germany they are called Margraves. Marquis is originally a French title. The first time we hear of marquises and marchionesses, is under Charlemagne, who created governors in Gascony under this denomination. The first that was created in England was Robert Vere, Earl of Oxford, made Marquis of Dublin by Richard II.

MARQUE (Letters of). The first letters of marque— or commissions marking the peculiar character of privateers —are believed to have been granted by Charles VI. of France, in the early part of the fifteenth century. Holland and Spain next adopted the privateering system; and our Queen Elizabeth, during the fierce and merciless war with Philip II., which was virtually ended by the destruction of the "Great Armada," covered the sea with privateers, who preyed not only upon Spanish commerce, but upon the vessels of neutral nations, and were, to all intents and purposes, "pirates." The "buccaneers" and "filibusters" of the Spanish Main, the stories of whose atrocities constitutes the most sanguinary page in the history of maritime warfare, plundered, massacred, tortured, and destroyed, under cover of letters of marque.

137

MASTER OF THE CEREMONIES.   The office
of master of the ceremonies was first instituted by James I.
The master of the ceremonies has to attend to the proper
presentation of ambassadors and other persons of quality to
the sovereign.   He also attends at court on all occasions of
state ceremonial, and has under him an assistant master, or
deputy. The gentleman who fills this office must necessarily
be a person of good address, and master of several languages.

MASTIFF. Anciently termed *Bandedog*, and an old
writer affirms that three were a match for a bear, and four
for a lion.   It appears that Great Britain was so noted for
this breed, that the Roman emperors appointed an officer in
this island, with the title of Procurator Cynegii, whose sole
business it was to breed, and transmit from hence to the
amphitheatre, such dogs as would prove equal to the combats exhibited at that place. The mastiff has been described
by naturalists, as a species of great size and strength, and a
very loud barker ; whence they have derived its name, mastiff, from *mase thefese ;* it being supposed to frighten away
robbers by its tremendous voice.

MAUNDAY THURSDAY.   This had its origin from
the Saxon *maund*, meaning a hand-basket, as being the day
on which provisions are given to the poor.   On this day in
England the Lord Almoner bestows the royal bounty on as
many poor persons as the sovereign is years old.   They
first attend Divine service, and afterwards receive clothes,
beef and bread, a sovereign, and as many silver pennies as
the sovereign has numbered years.

MAYDAY. It is most probable that this originated
with the northern nations, as their winters lasted from
138

October till April, and they had a custom of welcoming
the splendour of the returning sun with dancing and feasting,
from joy that a better season had arrived for fishing and
hunting. The Romans had their calends of May, when
they sacrificed to Flora, the goddess of flowers. It is not
unusual, in the present age, to see men, women, and children
go "Maying," as they term it, to cull the flowers of the hawthorn, or May-tree. Queen Elizabeth used to keep May-
games at Greenwich.

MAYORS (Lord). The word Mayor, comes from the
ancient English *maier*, able or potent, of the verb may or can.
Richard I., 1189, first changed the bailiffs of London into
mayors ; by whose example others were afterwards appointed.
The title of "lord" is said to have been first annexed to
that of mayor in the time of Richard II. This happened
in consequence of Walworth, mayor of London, having with
a blow of his dagger stunned the celebrated Wat Tyler, and
brought him to the ground (whom the King's attendants
instantly despatched), in a conference which Tyler had with
that monarch in Smithfield, 1381. But if the mayor gained
a new title by this transaction, his conduct was not at all
honourable. The king had agreed to have an interview
with Tyler ; and the mayor ought not to have acted as an
assassin on the occasion.

MAYPOLE. It was originally a custom for the clergyman of a parish, on the 1st of May, to lead his parishioners
to a neighbouring wood, and return in triumph with a long
pole, bedecked with flowers, boughs, and other emblems of
spring, around which they would dance and amuse themselves,
strewing flowers, etc., when it was set up. The morris
dance became introduced into the May games, in which

139

there was formerly a king and queen of the May, subsequently the king of the May was disused and Maid Marian
was sole sovereign or queen of the May, and it was usual
for the churchwardens to pay her for her trouble. When
a clown undertook the character, he received the title
of Malkin, or Maukin. (See *Morris Dance.*)

MEAT (Names of dead and alive). When William the
Conqueror came to the throne, he would only allow the
French language to be spoken at court, from which circumstance it is that we call animals kept for food by one name
while alive, and another when dead : this is however peculiar
to England. The names of our animals when alive, are of
Saxon origin, but when dead are of French. The Saxon
ox, calf, sheep, pig, etc., is in French, beef, veal, mutton,
pork, etc, and the only difference in the English language
is a slight alteration in the spelling.

MERRY ANDREW. A person named Andrew Borde,
a quack doctor, who was very popular in England in 1547,
and a sort of physician to Henry VIII., used to harangue
the populace with great wit and humour from the hustings
of his booth, in order to sell his nostrums. Thus Andrew,
by his merriment, drew crowds of people together ; therefore
quacks and buffoons have ever since been called by this name.

MICHAELMAS. The 29th of September. This day
is dedicated to St. Michael the archangel, and is so called
because of the mass celebrated in his honour by the Roman
Catholic Church on this day. It is supposed to have been
observed by Christians from the number of churches built
on high hills being dedicated to that saint, particularly in

140

Cornwall, of which St. Michael's Mount is an illustrative example.

MIDLENT SUNDAY. Is the middle or fourth Sunday in Lent, and was formerly called the Sunday of the Five Loaves, the Sunday of Bread, and the Sunday of Refreshment, in allusion to the gospel appointed for this day. It was also named Rose Sunday, from the pope's carrying a golden rose in his hand, which he exhibited to the people in the streets as he went to celebrate the eucharist, and at his return. On this day, in the south of Spain, children of all ranks, those of the poor in the street, and such as belong to the better classes in their houses, appear fantastically decorated, not unlike the English chimney sweepers on May-day, with caps of gilt and coloured paper.

MILLET. A grain used for puddings, which grows naturally in India, but is cultivated in Europe very successfully.

MINCE PIES. The dishes mostly in vogue among the ancient Christians for breakfast and supper on Christmas-day were, first, a boar's head stuck with rosemary, with a large apple or orange in its mouth, then plum porridge and mince pies; all of which they considered a test of orthodoxy, as these esculents were held in abomination by the Jews. The mince pies were made long, in imitation of the cretch, or manger, in which Christ was laid (See *Yule Cake*).

MISTLETOE (Kissing under). This is a custom at Christmas of immemorial antiquity. It was practised in

141

Druidical times.   The misletoe is, therefore, not introduced into churches, like the holly, for it is considered too carnal for the spiritual temple.   According to the *Edda* (or Scandinavian Bible), the mistletoe-berry seems to have been the forbidden fruit ; and Eve must have kissed Adam in Eden under the mistletoe-bough, when she presented him with a berry.

MOLOCH.   A dreadful idol god of the East.   It was a statue with the head of an ox, and the hands stretched out as a man's, who opens his hands to receive something from another.   It was hollow within.   There were seven chapels raised, before which the idols were erected.   The devotee that offered a fowl, or a young pigeon, went into the first chapel ; if a sheep or a lamb, he went into the second ; a ram, into the third ; a calf, into the fourth ; a bullock, into the fifth ; an ox, into the sixth ; but he only who offered his own son, went into the seventh chapel, and kissed the idol. The child was placed before the idol, and a fire made inside the statue till it became red hot.   Then the priest took the child, and put him into the glowing hands of Moloch, and lest the parents should hear his cries, they beat drums to drown the noise.

MONARCHS (Surnames of).   Surnames were originally considered nicknames (in imitation of the Romans).   The first on record is King Alfred, who was called the Great. His son Edward was called the Elder, from being the first of that name ; Edgar, the Peaceable ; Edward (his successor) the Martyr ; Edmund, Ironside ; Harold, Harefoot ; Edward, the Confessor ; William I., the Bastard ; William II., Rufus ; Henry II., Plantagenet ; Richard I., Cœur de Lion ; John, Lackland ; Edward I., Longshanks ; Henry

142

IV., Canker Bolingbroke; Henry V., Harry Monmouth; Richard III., Crookback; Mary, Bloody Queen, etc.

MONDAY (Black). This has been applied to the Monday after a vacation, when youth returned to their respective schools; but the true origin is from Easter Monday, 1351, when Edward III. invaded France, on which day a dreadful storm of wind, rain, lightning, and hail arose. The hailstones were so prodigiously large, that they instantly killed 6000 of his horses, and 1000 of his best troops.

MONSEIGNEUR. This is a French word (*mon*, my, *seigneur*, lord). It was originally applied to the saints of the Catholic Church; but subsequently, certain high clerical dignitaries and nobles arrogated the title. Under the old French monarchy, the eldest son of the dauphin was styled Monseigneur, without any additional title.

MONTHS (Derivation of). *January*, is derived from Janus, a heathen deity, who was supposed to preside over the gates of heaven. He was represented with two faces, one looking towards the old year, the other towards the new. He was the first king of Italy, and the ancient Romans used to give the doors in their houses the name of Janua. The heathens of old used to celebrate the festival of new year's day, with every sort of veneration, and the primitive Christians kept it as a solemn fast, which is still partially observed in England. The Saxon name of January means "Wolf month," as the wolves at that season are desperately mischievous, from being unable to procure food. *February*. This word is derived from Februo, to purify, because the feasts of purification were celebrated at this season; but the Romans

143

. offered sacrifice to their goddess Februo for the spirits of their departed friends. In the Saxon language its name implies " colewort," or " spring-wort," because worts begin to spring about this time. *March.* This was originally the first month in the Roman year, and was dedicated to Mars, the god of war. Its Saxon name means " lengthening month," as the days begin visibly to lengthen ; rather, the days begin to be longer than the nights. *April,* is so called from *aperio,* which signifies to open, because nature now begins to reveal its hidden charms, and expand its beauties. In Saxon it was called " Oster," or " Easter Monat," because the feast of their goddess Eastre was then celebrated. *May.* This month was so named by Romulus, the founder of Rome, in honour of Maia, the mother of Mercury ; but its Saxon name signifies "three milkings," as they then milked their cows three times daily. *June,* was so termed by the Romans, in honour of Mercury, who was represented as a juvenile figure, to which they applied the word Junius. The Saxons called it " weyd," or " meadow " month, because their cattle were then turned out to feed in the meadows. *July* This was originally called by the Romans Quintilis, being the fifth month of their year, but was changed to Julius in honour of Julius Cæsar. In Saxon it was called " hay month," as they used to cut their hay at this season. *August,* was anciently called by the Romans, Sextis, or sixth month from March ; but in honour of Augustus Cæsar, second emperor of Rome, it was changed to August. The Saxons called it " arn-monat," or " barn-month," because they then filled their barns. *September,* was derived from Septem, the seventh month of the Roman year, and *imber,* which means a shower. The Saxons named it "grist-month," as they then carried their new corn to the mill. *October.*

144

This was the eighth month of the Roman year, reckoning from March. In Saxon, its name denotes "wine-month," because their grapes were then pressed to make wine; or "winter-month," as the winter commenced with the full moon of this month. *November.* This word is derived from *novem* and *imber*, or the ninth month of the Roman year. In Saxon, it was sometimes called "blot-monat," or "blood-month," from the number of cattle slain and stored for winter provisions; others named it "windy-month," because of the high winds common in this month. And *December*, from *decem*, the tenth month of the Roman year; the Saxons called it "winter-month," from the intensity of the cold, or "holy-month," on account of the nativity of Christ.

MORRIS DANCE is so called in imitation of a Moorish dance, as sarabands, chacous, etc., usually performed with castanets, tambours, etc., by young men in their shirts, with bells at their feet, and ribbons of various colours tied round their arms and flung across their shoulders. (See *May Pole.*)

MOURNING. The origin of mourning is unknown, but it must have been a very ancient custom, as Abraham mourned for Sarah, Isaac for his father, and the children of Israel for Moses. On the death of a friend, it is customary in most European countries to wear black, this colour being deemed the most solemn. In eastern Asia, and other parts, different colours are preferred; for instance, the Chinese, ancient Romans, and Spartans wore white, emblematical of their friends being in paradise, clad in robes of pure white. The Egyptians wear yellow, in allusion to the fall and decay of the leaf. The Ethiopians

L   145

wear brown, implying that the body has returned to its native brown earth. The Turks wear violet, in allusion to the early spring-flower, or hope on one side, and sorrow on the other. Some of the islanders in the Pacific wear grey, implying that grey hairs go down to the grave in sorrow. The sovereigns of England select purple for mourning, and in France the chancellor never wears mourning at all.

MULTIPLICATION TABLE. The abacus, or counting table, among mathematicians, was a little table strewed over with dust, on which they drew their schemes and figures. Pythagoras, who is supposed to have been a pupil of Thales, is said to have invented the multiplication table.

MUMMERS. Mumming was one among the numerous pristine sports kept up at Christmas, and in the reign of Elizabeth, extended even to royalty. Among the common people, it principally consisted in the exchange of clothes between men and women, and corks were burnt to blacken their faces, to prevent a recognition when they went from house to house to partake of Christmas cheer. The custom of mummers is still preserved in some parts of the country— Somerset, etc.

MUSES (Nine). In mythology, the nine muses are described as the daughters of Jupiter and Mnemosyne, or Memory. The first, Clio (which means glory or renown), presided over history ; second, Thalia (blooming or flourishing), presided over comedy ; third, Melpomene (attracting), the muse of tragedy ; fourth, Terpsichore (amusing or rejoicing the heart), muse of dancing ; fifth, Euterpe (agreeable or pleasing), muse of instrumental music ; sixth, Erato, (the amiable or lovely), muse of light or amorous poetry ;

146

seventh, Polyhymnia (signifying a multitude of songs), muse of singing, rhetoric, etc. ; eighth, Urania (celestial), muse of astronomy ; ninth, Calliope (voice), muse of rhetoric, heroic poetry, and eloquence.

MUSICAL SIGNS. The seven musical signs—ut, re, mi, fa, sol, la, sa—invented by the Benedictine monk, Guido Aretino, are the first syllables of some words contained in the first stanza of a Latin hymn, composed in honour of St. John the Baptist, which runs thus :—

*Ut*queant laxis,	*Sol*ve polluti,
*Re*sonare fibris,	*La*bii reatum,
*Mi*ra gestorum,	*Sa*ncte Joannes.
*Fa*muli tuorum,	

MYTHOLOGY. Many characters and events of the greatest note, recorded in mythology, had their origin in the Bible, which, in process of time, became grossly corrupted. The story of Pandora's box was founded on the fall of Adam and Eve ; Neptune, or god of the sea, was founded on the history of Noah, as well as that of Janus and Bacchus ; Janus being represented with two faces (see *January*), was descriptive of Noah, who lived both before and after the flood ; and Bacchus, being the god of wine, was an allusion to Noah, who first discovered it. There is also a great resemblance in the history of Bacchus to that of Moses. The labours of Hercules were founded on the stories of Jonah, David, Samson, and Joshua. Vulcan was a corruption of Tubal-Cain, who first taught the art of working in iron and brass. The account of the Titans, or giants, was emblematic of the attempt to build the Tower of Babel.

N.

NAMES. The Jews, Arabs, Persians, and other eastern nations, usually gave their daughters the names of those objects mostly prized by them; for instance, Susanna means a lily; Hedessa a myrtle; Tamar a palm-tree; Rhoda a rose; Sophia, wisdom; etc. We find it recorded also in the Book of Job, that there were no females found so fair as his children, which is particularly expressed by their names. By Jemima, his first daughter, is meant "the day," fair as the day, "child of beauty," "*dove*," or "fairest woman in the east;" Keziah means "fragrant spice," or "fragrant as cassia," which was a spice of great repute in early ages; this shows also, how fond the Arabians were of naming women after the most beautiful productions of the earth. Kerenhappuch means "horn of paint," "child of beauty," or "blooming fairer than the tint of vermilion." Or it might have been from the beautiful black colour of the hair and eyebrows; or horn of stibium, which was an ornamental colouring to make the eyebrows perfectly black, which colour they considered the most beautiful.

NAUTILUS. This is a fish with a shell shaped like a ship; it has eight legs of different lengths, which it uses as oars and rudders, whilst a skinny membrane serves as a sail. It is supposed that the idea of sailing boats was first suggested to man by this fish. It obtains its name from the Greek *naus*, a ship, or, *nautes*, a sailor.

NEMESIS. One of the infernal deities, daughter of Nox, the goddess of vengeance, always prepared to punish impiety, and at the same time liberally to reward the good and virtuous. She was prepared to punish the crimes of the

148

wicked by land or by sea, and is represented with the helm and wheel in her hands.

NEWSPAPERS. It appears from Suetonius that a species of journal, or newspaper, was first used among the Romans, during the government of Julius Cæsar, who ordered that the acts and harangues of the senators should be copied out and published, as our parliamentary debates are printed, for the benefit of the public at the present day. This practice was continued to the time of Augustus, who discontinued it. It was, however, resumed in the reign of Tiberius. The title, Gazette, which was applied to a paper that came out every month (about 1600) in Venice, is supposed to be derived from *gazetta,* a small piece of Italian money, in value about a penny. There are some who think the name is from the Latin *gaza,* signifying a little treasury of news. The first English newspaper was *The English Mercurie,* printed at London, 1588, and the first number of the *London Gazette* was published November 7th, 1665. Gazettes were first introduced in France 1631; in Leipsig, 1715; in Amsterdam, 1732; at the Hague, 1735; at Cologne, 1756; and the Lower Rhine, 1764.

NINEPENNY LOVERS. Until the year 1696, when all money not milled was called in, a ninepenny piece of silver was as common as sixpences or shillings; and these ninepences were usually bent, which bending was called, *To my love, and from my love;* and such pieces the ordinary youths gave or sent their sweethearts as tokens of love.

NUT-CRACK NIGHT, by which name Hallowe'en is known in the north of England. At this entertainment nuts are placed on the bars of the grate or in the embers, one nut being named after the girl and the other after her lover. If the nut jumps away, it is supposed, the lover will prove unfaithful ; if it begins to blaze, he has a regard for the fair sorceress, and if both burn together, they will be married.

NUTMEGS. These are hollow if grated at one end, and solid by beginning at the other. This apparent anomaly is owing to the peculiar structure of the fibres of this fruit, and ought to be carefully observed by the consumers of it, who should never begin to grate it at the stalk end, or they will find it hollow throughout ; but by beginning at the other end, it will prove perfectly solid.

NUTHOOK. This word anciently expressed contempt ; and from the following note on the Merry Wives of Windsor, "thief" was the precise meaning of the word — " Nuthook was a term of reproach in cant strain ; and, 'if you run the nuthook's humour on me,' is, in plain English, 'if you say I am a thief.'" "His fingers are like fish-hooks," is still a vulgar phrase, often applied to people of a pilfering disposition.

O.

O YES! O YES! O YES! This exclamation by the public crier is derived from the French word *oyez*, which signifies hear ye, or listen ; and was originally adopted to command attention and silence, particularly in a court of justice.

OAK-APPLE DAY. An opinion has long prevailed, that Charles II. concealed himself in an oak-tree after the battle of Worcester, and branches or leaves are worn in

150

commemoration of his preservation. But this is evidently a mistake, as the battle of Worcester was fought on the 3rd of September, 1651, when Charles fled from the field, and concealed himself in a pollard oak-tree near Boscobel House, from whence he escaped to Normandy. He subsequently landed in England on the 29th of May (which was his birthday), when the royalists displayed branches of oak, as being partly instrumental to his restoration. Hence the custom of wearing oak on that day.

OATHS. An oath is considered, in a legal sense, the most solemn action that a person can undertake, whereby he calls his God to witness his communication, and that he may expect everlasting misery if he pervert the truth. Legal oaths end with " So help me God," when the party who is sworn kisses a Bible or Testament, a book emblematic of his faith or religion. The custom of kissing the New Testament, as an oath, took its rise among the Jews, who used to swear with the book of the law open before them, holding a parchment, with a passage of Scripture written on it, in their hands. After this, they ventured to touch the book, and then reverentially kiss it. In subsequent ages, Christians used to swear by the Sacrament of the Lord's Supper. This was in vogue so late as the fourth century.

OIL. In the earliest ages, it was customary among the Jews to anoint with oil those appointed to hold high offices ; and they considered it almost indispensable. They also thought it a sovereign remedy against all diseases in the human frame, as well as against the bite of any venomous animal. Washing the feet and anointing with oil, were the first civilities offered on entering a friend's house. This office was usually performed by the slaves. The anointing of kings with oil, so often mentioned in Scripture, appears to have been in early use in Britain; as, on the authority of Geoffrey of Monmouth, we are informed that our renowned king Arthur was a king anointed; and, by the testimonies of Bede and Malmesbury, we are assured of the existence of the custom not long after that period. The oil was consecrated for the purpose.

OPHIOLATREANISM. This means serpent worship, which has prevailed, perhaps without a single exception, over the whole surface of the inhabited earth. The serpent, by some nations, is regarded as an evil, by others as a good deity. The serpent may be traced in the ceremonials of the worship of Egypt, Greece, and Rome. In Britain, it was anciently held in high veneration, and the archdruid possessed a talisman called the serpent's egg; all their temples were built in a serpentine form. In the East, they are regarded by some with feelings of horror; by others, with sentiments of devotion.

ORDNANCE SURVEY. The trigonometrical survey of England was commenced by General Roy, in 1784, continued by Colonel Colby, and completed by Colonel James, in 1856. The publication of the maps commenced in 1819, under the direction of Colonel Mudge. The survey of Ireland has been completed; that of Scotland is not yet published.

OVENS. In various parts of the East, instead of what we call ovens, they dig a hole in the ground, in which they insert an earthen pot, which having sufficiently heated, they stick their cakes to the inside, and, when baked, remove them and supply their places with others. In cities and villages,

152

where there are public ovens, the bread is usually leavened; but in other parts, as soon as the dough is kneaded, it is made into thin cakes, which are either baked upon the coals, or in a shallow earthen vessel like a frying-pan. The Arabs about mount Carmel make a fire in a great stone pitcher, and when it is heated, mix meal and water, which they put on the outside of the pitcher, and this soft paste, spreading itself upon it, is baked in an instant, and the bread comes off as thin as wafers. Dr. Shaw and Rev. Bourne Hall Draper, are the authorities.

OYER AND TERMINER. These words, as applied to courts, mean courts for the trial of offences against the laws, or "criminal" courts. The words are from the old law French, and mean *to hear and determine.* The court *hears* the charge against a prisoner, and what he has to say in his defence, and then *determines* what shall be done about the matter.

P.

PACIFIC OCEAN. So named by Magellan, the great navigator, after passing through the dangerous straits which bear his name. He sailed nearly four months towards the north-west, without discovering land, and suffered the greatest distress in his voyage before he discovered the Ladrone Islands; but he enjoyed such delightful weather during the whole time, and such favourable winds, that he called this ocean the Pacific, which name it still retains.

PALM SUNDAY. Is the Sunday before Easter, and was so called from Christ's entry into Jerusalem, when the multitudes who came to the Passover, strewed branches of

153

palms and other trees before Him, with acclamations and hosannas.   The practice of carrying palms, flowers, etc., is still observed in popish countries.   Also observed in England by people going out for what is termed palm, even in London.

PANCAKE BELL.   A custom prevails in Haden to ring what is called the pancake-bell on Shrove Tuesday. All the apprentices in the town, whose indentures terminate before the return of the above day, assemble in the belfry of the church at eleven o'clock, and, in turn, toll the tenor bell for an hour, at the sound of which all the housewives in the parish commence frying pancakes.   The sexton, who is present, receives a small fee from each lad.

PANTHEIST.   This term is applied to a class of philosophical atheists who regard the universe as God— who worship nature instead of nature's God.   The word is derived from the Greek *pan*, "the whole;" *Theos*, "God."

PANTOMIME is derived from a Greek word, signifying "imitate," and properly refers to a species of theatrical entertainment where the performance is carried on in dumb show.

PARLIAMENT.   The first Parliament in England was held in 1116, but the assembly as at present constituted was convened, according to Magna Charta, in 1215.   It is supposed that the Commons of England began to sit in a separate house about 1260.   Opposition parties were regularly formed in 1620.   "The word "parliament" is derived from the French *parler*—"to speak;" reference

154

being made to the power which every member has of speaking his mind for the public good. (See *Commons.*)

PARTHIANS. These were supposed to be the ancient Persians, a name derived from the Hebrew, implying horsemen, as these people were particularly noted for their superior management of horses and the bow and arrow. They are also classed with the Elamites, Ælam being the original name of Persia.

PASSOVER. This is one of the principal and most solemn festivals of the Jews, in commemoration of their miraculous deliverance, when the Almighty smote the first-born of the Egyptians, and their escape from bondage. It lasts eight days, during which they carefully abstain from all fermented liquors, and eat unleavened bread, or cakes made of flour and water; but the wealthy add eggs and sugar, similar to our pancakes. (See *Easter.*)

PATERNOSTER ROW. So named, according to Stow, from the number of text writers who dwelt there, who wrote and sold the Paternoster, Ave, Creed, Graces, and other publications of a similar character.

PATRIARCH. A patriarch is a father and a ruler of a family, and was applied chiefly to those who lived before Moses, who were both priests and princes.

PAVING. According to historians, the ancient city of Babylon and the streets of Carthage were both paved; but the Romans had no paved streets or roads until the censorship of Appius Claudius, under whom was constructed the celebrated Roman road, known as the Appian Way. Paving was not practised in London until the end

155

of the eleventh century. In the year 1417, we read that Henry V., impressed with the deep and dangerous state of the Holborn roadway, directed two vessels to be employed at his expense in bringing stones for mending and paving that highway. The present system of macadamising—so named from its projector, M'Adam—was introduced into London in 1824.

PAWNBROKER'S SIGN. This sign was taken from that of the Italian bankers, who were the first to open loan-shops in England for the relief of temporary distress. The three balls, or pills, are the arms of the Lombard merchants, who, having accumulated an immense property, built a great portion of the street so named from themselves

PEERS OF THE REALM. The nobility of this kingdom is divided into Dukes, Marquises, Earls, Viscounts, and Barons, and are generally and collectively called Peers of the Realm. The reason they are called peers is, that notwithstanding a distinction of dignities in our nobility, yet in all public actions they are equal; as in their votes of parliament, etc. The appellation seems to have been borrowed from France, from those twelve peers instituted by Charlemagne in that kingdom, and called *Pares, vel Patricii Franciæ.*

PEG TANKARDS. The Saxons were remarkable for immoderate drinking. Dunstan endeavoured to checkt his vicious habit, but durst not totally obstruct their intemperance. He introduced, therefore, the custom of marking, or pegging, their cups. These tankards had in the inside a row of eight pins, one above another, from top to bottom, and held two quarts. The first that drank was to empty

156

the tankard to the first peg, or pin , the second to the next, and so on, by which means the pins being so many (half-pint) measures, be made them all drink alike. It is through these tankards that we are enabled to trace the origin of some of our common proverbs. When we wish to express an intention of checking any obtrusive conduct in a person, we say that he must be taken "*a peg lower.*" If a person is not in good spirits, we say he is "*a peg too low.*" When a person is slightly inebriated, we say he is "*in a merry pin;*" or if overstepping the rules of decorum, and is taking greater liberties than prudence will allow, we say he is getting on "*peg by peg*" Another method of measuring the draught of each man was by hoops being marked in a drinking pot. Shakespeare makes Jack Cade say to his followers, "There shall be in England seven halfpenny loaves sold for a penny —*the three hooped pot shall have ten hoops*, and I will make it felony to drink small beer." From thence is derived the phrase of "*Carouse the hunter's hoop.*"

PELL MELL. Pall Mall was originally a place where people used to meet and play with malls and balls. It is derived from the Latin *pila*, a ball, and *malleus*, a mallet ; the mall was a walk, to which the people resorted to enjoy the game, and the words were anciently pronounced pell mell, from the people of every grade of society resorting thither.

PETER'S PENCE. An annual tax of one penny, or, as some say, of one shilling, imposed on every family in England, and paid to the popes, for the maintaining of an English college at Rome. It was established by Offa, king of Mercia, 755, and after the union of the seven kingdoms,

157

was collected throughout all England. It was abolished at the Reformation, in the reign of Henry VIII.

PHALANX. The Grecian phalanx was a body of troops, armed with spears, and formed in a square. The phalanx consisted first of 4000 men, but Philip of Macedon, doubled it, and afterwards it was quadrupled. The men stood close together, with their shields locked, and spears extended.

PHARISEES. This name is derived from *pharas,* a Hebrew word, which signifies separation, because they separated themselves from their Jewish brethren, and affected a higher degree of holiness, in consequence of which they were reverenced by the lower classes. The title was mostly applied to the rich and independent, those of the lower grade being termed the multitude, the people, etc. Their religion consisted principally in the observance of external ceremonies, oblations, and purifications : they fasted often, and made long prayers in public places ; and were such strict observers of the Sabbath, that they considered it wicked to heal the sick on that day. They believed in the resurrection, and in the existence of angels and spirits ; but by the former they meant the transmigration of the souls of good men into other bodies.

PHILIPPICS. The name given to the orations of Demosthenes against Philip, king of Macedon, to rouse the Athenians against Philip, and guard against his crafty policy, hence applied to any violent or bitter declamation against a person. They are esteemed the masterpieces of that orator. Cicero's philippics cost him his life ; Mark Antony having been so irritated with them, that when he arrived at the triumvirate, he procured Cicero's murder, cut off his head, and stuck it up in the very place where the orator delivered the philippics.

PHŒNIX. The origin of the fable of the phœnix is explained thus :—In the Holy Land, and in most eastern countries, the palm-tree is, by way of distinction, called the Phœnix, in consequence of its great utility, and Palestine could scarcely be said to be inhabited without it. When the tree grows old, it is cut down and burned to ashes, from which ashes springs a young palm-tree, or phœnix.

PHRASES (Singular). The following terms were used in some parts of England in former times, for pecuniary fines, etc., and have the subjoined import :—" Danegeld:"— A sum first paid to the Danes to leave England at peace ; but continued as a tax for some little time after the Conquest. " Murdrum:"—A fine imposed upon a place wherein a murder had been committed ; or for not producing the murderer if he had fled thither. "Lastage:"—A compensation for liberty to bring goods to markets, or to carry them where the owner thought proper, paid by the last. " Passage:"—Money paid for the passing to and fro of persons and goods, on common shores, landing places, etc. " Pontage:"—Toll for passing over bridges with horses, carriages, etc. ; or under them in boats, or other vessels. " Murage." —A duty collected upon carts or horses passing through a town, for building or repairing its walls. " Picage:"—Money paid for breaking up the ground to erect booths, stalls, etc., in fairs. (See *Scot and Lot*).

PILGRIM. One who travels to distant places and countries on some religious errand.

PIN MONEY. It is most probable that this term had its origin in the simplicity of our forefathers, before pins were so numerous as they now are ; as, in their bargains, it was usual to make a present to the wife and children of the person with whom they dealt, and this was termed pins, or pin-money, from which we may infer that the term has been similarly applied to the allowance which a husband makes to his wife for her own individual use.

PINS. Their first mention in English history is in 1483, when their importation was prohibited under a statute of Richard III Before that time many ingenious contrivances were adopted for the purpose of fastening the dress, and the fulfilment of the other offices which are usually assigned to this article. Until the introduction of pins, ladies made use of ribands, loops, laces, tags, hooks and eyes, and skewers of wood, bone, brass, silver, and gold. The ingenious and expeditious method of making pins by machinery now in use was invented about 1824.

PIPING HOT. This expression is taken from the custom of a baker's blowing his pipe, or horn, in villages to let the people know his bread is just drawn, and consequently "hot" and light.

PLANTAGENET. No positive account is given as to the origin of this word, which was first borne by Henry II. But it is supposed that his father, the Earl of Anjou, whose conscience smote him for some bad action, went on a pilgrimage to the Holy Land, where he was soundly scourged with broom twigs, or *planta genista,* which grew there in abundance ; after which he took the name of Plantagenet, or Broomstalk, which his noble posterity still retain. Among the badges of Richard II. were the sun in splendour, and the pod of the *planta genista* (hence Plantagenet), or broom, with which the robe of his monumental effigy is covered.

PLATINUM. This is found in South America and Asiatic Russia. When pure, it resembles silver, though not so bright. Its beauty, ductility, and its not being easily rusted, make it little inferior to gold or silver.

PLEASE REMEMBER THE GROTTO. Those who have so often heard this common street request made by London children, on old St. James's day (the 5th of August), will possibly be surprised when we tell them that in the humble grotto, formed of oyster-shells, lit up with a votive candle, we have a memorial of the world-renowned shrine of St. James at Compostella.

PLEASE THE PIGS. This, with a slight alteration, was an old Roman Catholic ejaculation—"An it please the pix," which is the box in which the host was carried.

PLOUGH MONDAY. Is the first Monday after Epiphany, and was observed by our ancestors by drawing a plough in procession on this day, indicating the period for renewing rural labours after Christmas. It is still observed in many parts of England, where they go from door to door begging plough-money, which they expend in the evening in merriment and feasting as a farewell holiday.

POISONED INSTRUMENTS OF WAR. The art of poisoning war implements appears to have been very ancient, as we read it in the book of Job, chap. vi. ver. 4. It was also practised by the Arabians, Moors, and people of other nations. Homer also states that Ulysses went to

Ephyra for poison to smear his brazen-pointed arrows. The Indians dip their arrows in the gall of asps and vipers, and other poisonous preparations, which fire the blood of the wounded, cause great pain and make the least wound mortal.

POLL TAX. In the year 1667, every subject was assessed by the head, namely :—a duke, £100, marquis, £80 ; baronet, £30 ; knight, £20; esquire, £10; and every simple person one shilling. This grievous tax was abolished by William III.

POPE. The appellation of pope (a father) was originally given to all Christian bishops, but was usurped solely by the bishops of Rome in the eleventh century, with whom it has remained ever since. Abbot, signifies the superior individual of a monastery or abbey. Friar, or brother, is a term common to the monks of all orders ; but generally confined to those monks who are not priests, for all in holy orders are termed fathers.

PORCELAIN. This word is derived from *pour cent années*, it being formerly believed that the materials of porcelain were matured under ground one hundred years. It is not known who first discovered the art of making it, but the manufacture has been carried on in China, at King-te-Ching, ever since the year 442. We first hear of it in Europe in 1581, and soon after this time it was known in England. The finest porcelain ware, known as Dresden China, was discovered by an apothecary's boy, named Boeticher, in 1700. Services of this ware have sometimes cost many thousand pounds each.

162

POSTS. Posts, in their present and improved state, are of very modern invention ; for, even in France, the first place of their adoption, they were, in 1619, still unprovided with a letter office. In the year 1635, the first regular establishment of the kind in England was formed. A private person projected, in 1683, the conveyance of letters by the penny post, throughout London and the suburbs. The custom of making pigeons the vehicle of postage still exists among the Turks, and in several eastern countries. The same winged messengers have been employed by the Dutch in sieges. Crows were sometimes used as letter carriers ; and Cecinna, a Roman knight, in the interest of Pompey, used to bring up young swallows, and send them as messengers to carry news to his friends.

POUNCE. Is gum sandaric reduced to a fine powder, and used to prevent the sinking of paper after the erasure of writing. It is procured, likewise, from the pulverized bone of the cuttle-fish.

PRESBYTERIAN. This term comes from the Greek word which signifies Senior or Elder. Calvin may be said to have been the founder of Presbyterianism, having first established that form of religion at Geneva, about the year 1541.

PRICKING FOR TEXTS. This means pricking, or opening the Bible at hazard, and endeavouring to extract from the passage which first catches the eye, something analogous to your situation. This superstitious custom prevails in the Greek Church. Mohammedans, especially those of Egypt, perform the same sort of ceremony with the Koran. Even in Scotland—a country in which Holy Writ is more venerated, perhaps, than in any other—the custom of "pricking for texts" for the purposes of augury, was common up to the present century.

PRIEST. A priest, means a person who is invested with holy orders, and has authority to preach, pray, and administer the sacrament. None are admitted to the priesthood under the age of twenty-four.

PRIMATE. A primate is an archbishop, who is invested with a jurisdiction over other bishops.

PRINCE'S MIXTURE. This term is not only applied to a favourite snuff. Prince's Island is celebrated among African cruisers for the bad weather so commonly met with near it, frequent and vexatious showers of rain, and gusts of wind, all which are quaintly termed by seamen, Prince's Mixture.

PROCRUSTES (Bed of). This expression is often used. Procrustes was a famous robber of Attica, remarkable for a cruel method of treating travellers by compelling them to lie down upon his bed; if they were larger than the bed, he would cut off enough to make them the same length ; if they were shorter, he would stretch them out. This monster was killed by Theseus, who served him as he had served his victims, making him fit his own bed.

PROPHET. A good man, inspired by the Almighty with power to foretell what will happen. Evangelist : an inspired writer, or messenger of good tidings ; a revealer of the gospel, etc. Apostle, implies a person or messenger sent on business of importance ; and by way of eminence, it is applied to those twelve disciples commissioned by Jesus Christ to preach His gospel. (*See Apostles.*)

164

Disciple means a person who follows any particular sect of people, either in religion, art, or science. Martyr means one who lays down his life for the sake of his religion, which he declares to be true; or who will undergo any punishment rather than renounce his opinion.

PROTESTANT. The word denotes all Christians who deny the pope's supremacy, and other doctrines of the Romish Church. It was first applied to those reformers in Germany who embraced and adhered to the doctrines of Martin Luther, because, in 1529, they protested against a decree of the Emperor Charles V., declaring that they appealed to a free council.

PULL HAIR AND HAIR, AND YOU'LL MAKE THE CARLE BALD. There is a story of Sertorius, mentioned by Plutarch, in his Life :—" he, to persuade his soldiers that counsel was more available than strength, causes two horses to be brought out ; the one poor and lean ; the other strong, and having a bushy tail. To the weak horse, he sets a strong, great, young man. To the strong horse, he sets a little weak fellow, each to pluck off his horse's tail. The latter, pulling the hairs one by one, in a space of time got off the whole tail, whereas, the young man, catching all the tail at once in his hands, fell a tugging with all his might, labouring to little purpose ; till at last he tired, and made himself ridiculous to the company."

PULLING BY THE NOSE. The origin of this affront is given by an old Scotch writer. When any freeman renounces his liberty, and makes himself bond or slave to any great man in his court, and makes tradition and delivering himself by giving one grip of the hair of his forehead, to the effect he may be maintained and defended by him hereafter—such bondman, if he reclaim his liberty, or happen to be fugitive from his master, may be *drawn* back again to servitude. From this custom arose the Scottish saying, when any boasteth and menaces, that he intends to take another by the nose.

PULLING EARS. Among the Romans it was a custom to pull or pinch the ears of witnesses, present at any transaction, that they might remember it when they were called to give in their testimony. Among the Athenians, it was a mark of nobility to have the ears bored ; and among the Hebrews and Romans this was a mark of servitude.

PUMP. This hydraulic machine is said to have been invented by Ctesibius, of Alexandria, about 120 B.C. ; but on what principle it was then constructed is not ascertained. The date of the invention of modern times is the commencement of the fifteenth century. The rise of water in the pump was long supposed to be due to the principle that nature " abhors a vacuum;" and the true reason—the pressure of the atmosphere—was not ascertained till the middle of the seventeenth century.

PUNCTUATION. It appears certain that the ancients were not acquainted with the use of any marks to assist the reader in ascertaining the sense of the author, but that he was left to discover it from the general tenor of the subject. The earliest printed books had no stops, but some arbitrary signs here and there, introduced according to the humour of the printer. The marks of punctuation now used were invented in the sixteenth and seventeenth centuries. The points in punctuation mark the length of pauses, thus :—

166

, This is a comma—here I stay
  While counting one upon my way.
; A semi-colon next I view ;
  Here I must stop and count one, two.
: A colon next I plainly see,
  And stop to count my one, two, three.
. A period now, which means still more ;
  I stop and count one, two, three, four.

PUNISHMENTS. The punishment of felons by death, with hanging upon the gallows, is very ancient. This was abolished by William the Conqueror, who appointed instead of it, pulling out eyes, cutting off hands or feet, and otherwise mutilating criminals, according to the extent of the offence, so that they might live and be a terror to others. This kind of punishment continued but a short time, for Henry I., in 1108, decreed, that for theft and robbery they should be hanged. The first nobleman beheaded was Waltheof, Earl of Northumberland, in 1075 Felons were also put to death by drowning, in the reign of Edward II.

Q.

QUAKERS. This sect of Protestants derived their appellation about the year 1650, when George Fox, a dissenting minister, being brought before two justices, he desired them to " tremble " at the word of the Lord. And his followers were afterwards denominated, in derision, " Quakers." The quakers exist nowhere but in this country, and in North America.

QUASSIA. This shrub, a native of Surinam, was named, in honour of a negro, Quassi, a doctor, who had discovered the virtue of the wood in curing the malignant fevers of that hot, marshy country.

167

QUEEN ANNE'S FARTHINGS. The popular stories of the great value of this coin are fabulous, although some few of particular dates have been purchased at high prices. The current farthing, with the broad brim, when in fine preservation, is worth £1. The common patterns of 1713 and 1714 are also worth £1. The two patterns, with Britannia under a canopy, and Peace on a car, R.R.R., are worth £2 2s. each. The pattern, with Peace on a car, is more valuable and rare, and worth £5.

QUILTING. This term is used to describe an American merry-making, when a party of women assemble to sew patches into a quilt. At the end of the day's work the bed-cover is suspended from the ceiling, the young men of the neighbourhood join the party, a fiddler seats himself on a flour barrel, and they dance and enjoy themselves until a late hour.

QUIZ AND QUIZZING. These words, which are only in vulgar or colloquial use, but which Webster traces to learned roots, originated in a joke. Daly, the manager of a Dublin playhouse, wagered that a word of no meaning should be the common talk and puzzle of the city in twenty-four hours. In the course of that time the letters, q. u. i. z. were chalked or posted on all the walls of Dublin with an effect that won the wagers.

R.

RACE PLATE. A bell was formerly the prize run for. Afterwards, a silver bowl or cup was given to the winner. This was the origin of the word plate, which is still used, though only money be given. (See *Bell.*)

RAINBOW. This is one of the most surprising of natural phenomena. The Hebrews called it the " Bow of God," and the Greeks the " Daughter of wonder." This heavenly sign is seen in the falling rain or dew, and not in the cloud whence that rain or dew proceeds. It is caused by a reflection and refraction of the sun's rays from the globular particles of rain. The face of this beautiful bow is tinged with all the primigenial colours in their natural order—namely, violet, indigo, blue, green, yellow, and red. It always appears in that part of the heavens opposite the sun.

RECTOR. A rector, means a clergyman who has the care and cure of a parish, possessing all the tithes, etc. ; but when the *prædial*, or great tithes, which mean those belonging to or growing on farms, are impropriate (that is, when the possessions of the church are in the hands of a layman), the parson is called a vicar, and the layman rector; consequently, a vicar implies the priest of a parish, the great tithes of which are appropriated and belong to some chapter, religious house, or layman, who receives them, and only allows the vicar the small tithes, or a suitable salary. The duties of rectors and vicars are to take care of the congregation, perform Divine service, marriages, christenings, burials, etc.

REGIUM DONUM, or royal gift, was an annual grant of public money, made by the British parliament, in aid of the maintenance of the Presbyterian clergy of Ireland It was instituted by William III., in 1690, remodelled in 1790, and abolished by the act, passed in 1869, for disestablishing the Irish Church.

REPEAL RING. The ring, known as the " love ring,"

is formed of the following stones :—Lapis lazuli, opal, verd antique, emerald. The "regard ring" by means of a similar arrangement, consisting of ruby, emerald, garnet, amethyst, ruby, and diamond Rings of this class have also been used for political purposes. During the agitation of the repeal question in Ireland, a popular ring was formed of the following settings :—Ruby, emerald, pearl, emerald, amethyst, and lapis lazuli. This was the "repeal ring."

REVERSION. The interest which the owner of an estate in land reserves to himself, after the expiration of a smaller interest, or one of a shorter duration, which he has granted to another person. For instance, if the owner of a fee-simple grants another an estate for life, the right which he has to have the property back on the death of the person to whom it is so granted, is his "reversion;" and the interest which a landlord retains in land which he has granted or let to a tenant for a limited period is his "reversion."

RIDING THE BLACK LAD. At Ashton-under-Lyne, on Easter Monday, a custom is observed, called "Riding the Black Lad," in which a straw effigy, formerly incased in armour, is carried round the town ; after which it is hung up and shot at, in commemoration, according to some, of an Assheton who, at the battle of Neville's Cross, carried off the royal standard from the tent of the Scottish king; according to other authorities, in execration of the conduct of one of the same family, who, in the reign of Henry VI., levied a heavy tax upon the inhabitants.

RINGLEADER. This expression originated at sea, in what is termed by the sailors a "round robin," in consequence of their writing their names on a circular piece

170

of paper, in order to prevent a knowledge of the first person who signed, and thus avoid the punishment which would otherwise fall on him who first attached his name to any mutinous document. Still it generally happens that the first who signs, takes the lead in any tumult or riot, from which he is called the ringleader.

RINGS. It is impossible to trace the origin of wearing rings, but it is supposed, that in early ages it was instituted as an emblem of authority and government ; for we read in the Bible that Pharaoh took his ring from his finger and presented it to Joseph, as a sign of vested authority. In conformity to ancient usage, the Christian Church adopted the ring in the ceremony of marriage, as a symbol of the authority with which the husband invested his wife. This was made of gold, which metal the ancients used as a symbol of love, the ring itself being an emblem of eternity, or love without end. Rings, it appears, were first worn in India, whence the practice descended to the Egyptians, thence to the Greeks, from whom it passed to the Romans and others. The wedding ring was placed on the fourth finger of the left hand, because it was believed that a small artery ran from this finger to the heart. This has been contradicted by experience ; but several eminent authors were formerly of this opinion, therefore they thought this finger the most proper to bear the pledge of love, that from thence it might be carried to the heart. Others are inclined to think that it was in consequence of this finger being less used than any other, and is more capable of preserving a ring from bruises. Family rings were formerly given away at a marriage, as wedding presents. There was also the espousal, as well as the wedding, ring. This was observed till 850,

171

when each continued separate.   In the Greek Church,
espousals and marriages were distinct services.   In the
former parties exchanged rings in pledge of mutual fidelity ;
but within the last few centuries this has been discontinued
in the Church of England.   The custom of wearing a ring
on the thumb is very ancient.   An alderman's thumb ring
is mentioned by Shakespeare, and also in the *"Northern
Lass,"* which was acted at the Globe and Blackfriars, in
1603 :—"A good man in the city wears nothing rich
about him, but the gout or a thumb-ring."

RINGS (Jimmal).   A singular sort of ring was adopted
by lovers of antique times.   They are called gimmal, or
jimmal, rings.   They were double, sometimes treble, with
joints or links by which they could be separated.   It is
from this peculiarity they seem to have obtained their
name ; as jimmer (a north country word) signifies hinges.
Others ascribe the name to Gemelli, twins.   They were also
called St. Martin's rings.   It was sometimes the practice for
lovers to wear each a link of these twin rings.   (See *Rings*
and *Rush Rings.*)

ROB PETER TO PAY PAUL.   This phrase arose in
the reign of Edward VI., when some lands of St. Peter, at
Westminster, were invaded by the great men of the court,
who allowed something out of them towards the repairs of
St. Paul's church, which gave rise to the proverb.

ROGATION SUNDAY.   This day takes its name
from the Latin *rogare*, to ask ; because on the three subsequent days, supplications were appointed by Mamertus,
Bishop of Vienna, in the year 469, to be offered up with

172

fasting to God, to avert some particular calamities that threatened his diocese.

ROLAND FOR AN OLIVER.   The origin of this phrase is said to be as follows :—In the court of Charlemagne were two pages, equally handsome and proficient in all the accomplishments of the age.   So evenly balanced were they in their attainments, that whatever feat of skill or dexterity might be performed by the one, would immediately be reproduced by the latter.   Hence there came to be no choice between them in popular estimation; and the saying, "to give a Roland for an Oliver," was used to express the fact that any action had been followed by its exact equivalent in return.

ROLLING THE STONE OF SISYPHUS.   Sisyphus was the son of Eolus.   Having displeased Jupiter, Death was sent to him as a punishment ; but Sisyphus was very crafty, and managed to bind Death, so that he could not escape.   This pleased mortals highly, for no one died. Pluto set him at liberty, and Sisyphus was given up to his power.   While dying, Sisyphus begged his wife to leave him unburied after death.   She did so, and he then complained to Pluto (who had charge of the abode of the dead) of his wife's unkindness, and asked permission to return to light, and reprove her for the neglect.   The request was granted, and Sisyphus went home, and finding himself once more in his own house, refused to leave it, but Mercury obliged him to obey.   Pluto was so angry at this trick, that he set him to rolling a mammoth stone up a hill—a never ending labour; for when, after great exertion, he got it to the top, down it would roll again to the bottom.

173

ROMANCE (Ancient).   In 1864, a paper was read to
the Society of Antiquaries upon an ancient papyrus (an
Egyptian plant and the paper made from it), which had
been after much difficulty, deciphered.   It is a story of three
hundred lines, relating the adventures of an Asiatic wanderer,
about B.C. 2400.   This person flees from the court of king
Ammenemoo I. into Ethiopia, where he is hospitably entertained, marries the daughter of a chief, and becomes a rich
man.   In his old age he longs to return to Egypt, and
writes to the king for pardon.   The king returns a gracious
answer, and a copy of his letter is given.   The adventurer
describes his return to Egypt, the awe with which the king's
presence inspired him ; the mistaken zeal of the courtiers,
who, fancying that the king is about to punish the fugitive,
cry out that he is guilty ; the turning of the tables by the
king, who pronounces him innocent, instals him in a splendid house with a handsome pension, continues to smile upon
him till the day of his death, and builds him a magnificent
tomb.   (See *Alexandrian Verse.*)

ROSE (Emblem of England).   During the wars between
the houses of York and Lancaster, persons took different
symbols.   Those who espoused the cause of Lancaster wore
a red rose, and those of York a white one.   This was desig-
nated the War of the Roses.   They originated with the descendants of Edward III., and continued till the reign of Henry
VII., who, after the battle of Bosworth Field, married the
daughter of Edward IV. of York, by which both houses
were united ; since which, the rose has remained the emblem of England.

ROSE (Under the).   Roses were not known in England
till the early part of the fifteenth century, when they were

174

brought from Italy and planted in these parts. As the Catholic religion then predominated, they were consecrated as presents from the pope of Rome, and were placed over the heads of those who came to confess, as symbols of secrecy. Hence the phrase—Under the rose.

RUBRIC. By this is meant certain directions given at the commencement, or in the course of the Liturgy, to point out how the several parts of the Church service should be performed. It derives its name from the Latin *rubrica*, red, as the directions were formerly written or printed with red ink, to distinguish them from the other parts. Liturgy means the forms of prayer, or ceremonies, used in public worship in the Church of England. In the Roman Church it means mass, but with us common prayer.

RULE THE ROAST. To rule the roast, is to govern, manage, or preside over. It was originally written roist, which signifies a tumult, and then implied to direct the rabble.

RUSH RINGS. Rings of rush were at one time in favour as betrothal gifts; and the ancient dames of two hundred years ago used to aver, " 'Twas a good world when such simplicity was used, and a ring of rush would tie as much love together as a gimmon of gold." (See *Wedding* and *Jimmal Rings.*)

ROYAL PREROGATIVE. In England the sovereign is the supreme magistrate. It is a maxim that he can do no wrong. He is the head of the Established Church, of the army and navy, and the fountain of office, honour, and privilege; but is subject to the laws, unless exempted by name. The royal prerogatives were greatly exceeded by several despotic sovereigns, such as Elizabeth, James I., and Charles I. Elizabeth used the phrase, "We, of our royal prerogative, which we will not have argued or brought in question" (1691). James I. told his parliament, "that as it was blasphemy to question what the Almighty could do of His power, so it was sedition to inquire what a king could do by virtue of his prerogative." These extreme doctrines were nullified by the revolution of 1688; and the exercise of the prerogative is now virtually subject to parliament.

RUMBALD FEAST. A very curious custom formerly existed among the Dover fishermen, who on their return from their expeditions, used to select eight of the finest whitings out of each boat, and devote the proceeds to the celebration of a feast on Christmas eve, which they termed a "rumbald;" in honour, as some conjecture, of the Irish saint Rumbald, who was supposed to have some connection with whitings, or "rumbalds" as they are still called in some parts of Kent.

S.

SABBATH. This word is from "Shabath," denoting rest, and the prime idea of the Sabbath, as an institution, is a total cessation of secular labour. The Christian Church adopted Sunday as its Sabbath-day in commemoration of the resurrection of Christ, which occurred on that day. Sunday, in its etymology, is wholly distinct from its religious attributes, the day having been so named because anciently dedicated to the worship of the sun.

SACRAMENT. This word, although used to denote the most solemn of Christian institutions, is of heathen origin, and anciently signified the oath taken by the Roman

176

soldiers, when they enrolled themselves under the banners of their leaders. Hence it came to be used for that solemn service of the Church, by which Christians pledge themselves to be faithful to the great Captain of their salvation.

SADDUCEES. This most ancient sect among the Jews, who separated themselves from their brethren, and their founder Zadoc, considered that there would be no future punishment, although he admitted that there was a God, who made the world, and governed it by His providence; but that rewards or punishments were applicable to the present life, for which purpose he enjoined the worship of the Deity, and obedience to His laws. His disciples rejected all the Scriptures except the Pentateuch. They would not believe in the existence of angels, spirits, or the resurrection They were few in number, but eminent for wealth and dignity.

SAINTS' DAYS. The heathens were highly delighted with the festivities of their gods, and were very reluctant to dispense with them; therefore, to hasten their conversion, the early Christians, after the persecution by the emperor Decius, substituted festivals to the saints and martyrs . hence, in order to obviate the festivals of the heathens, those of Christian saints, etc , were introduced in their stead; such as keeping up Christmas sports instead of bacchanalia, saturnalia, etc.; celebrating May-day with flowers instead of floralia, etc.; the festivals of the Virgin Mary, John the Baptist, etc., instead of the usual solemnities when the sun entered the signs of the zodiac. By these means the Christians made a vast number of converts; but it must be admitted that they could not increase the solemnity of their religion. St. Paul strongly advised that instead of celebrating their festivals, they should devote themselves to the devout and social use of psalmody and prayer.

SALUTATIONS. The use of "Your humble servant," came first into England on the marriage of queen Mary, daughter of Henry IV. of France, which is derived from *"votre tres humble serviteur."* The usual salutation before that time was, " God help you," " God be with you ; " and among the vulgar, " How dost do ?" with a thump on the shoulder.

SANCTUARY. Superstition in past ages drove men as a last resource to shelter themselves in the temples, and to set the sacredness of the place and the vengeance of the gods between them and the cruelty of their enemies. This right of sanctuary became in the Catholic Church an established privilege and a source of revenue and power. Nor were the ecclesiastics content to consider this immunity confined to sacred edifices ; they created sanctuaries in other districts of their diocese, or procured the royal sanction for doing so. Thus, in the north-gate ward of Canterbury, it is said that St. Augustine procured of king Ethelbert the privilege of making the borough of Stablegate free from "all manner of public or private imposition, and to be a sanctuary or place of refuge for criminals ;" so that if thieves, murderers, or any other notorious offenders, though they were indicted, yet if they could get thither, should be under the power and protection of the archbishop only, and be as safe as if they were in a church. It was to this state of things that ancient London owed its Alsatia in the precincts of Whitefriars, and its little sanctuary in Westminster, besides those other strongholds of crime. the Mint, the

Minories, the Clink in Southwark, the Sanctuary in St. Martin's-le-Grand, and various others, which were not finally suppressed by the legislature till 1697.

SANDWICHES. Lord Sandwich, when Minister of State, having passed twenty-four hours at a public gaming-table, was so absorbed in play during the whole time, that he had no subsistence but a bit of beef between two slices of toasted bread, which he ate without quitting the game. This new dish was afterwards, and is to this day, called by the name of the minister who invented it.

SAW. This useful instrument had its origin from the circumstance of the jaw-bone of a snake being used to cut through a piece of wood, which succeeded so well, that the operator made a saw of iron, an account of which was displayed in a painting found among the ruins of Herculaneum.

SCOT AND LOT. This term signifies a customary contribution laid upon all subjects according to their ability. *Scot* comes from the French word *escot—i.e. symbolum*, a shot. *Scot*, says Camden, is still used in the sense of equal reckoning; for when good-fellows meet at a tavern or alehouse, they, at parting, call for a shot, scot, or reckoning; and he is said to go *scot free* that pays not his part or share towards it.

SCREW PROPELLER. This is simply the Archimedian screw reduced to a single turn. In the year 1785, J. Bramah patented "a wheel similar to the fly of a smoke-jack, or the sail of a windmill." This wheel was attached to the stern of the vessel, and driven by a steam engine.

The Americans had several variations of the Archimedian screw in use by the year 1816, and it soon became equally common in England. In 1823, Mr. Delisle produced a five threaded screw propeller; and Mr. Perkins, in the year 1825, invented an arrangement with double blades, one before the other, which were only partially immersed.

SCYLLA AND CHARYBDIS. The first was a famous rocky promontory, near the Straits of Messina, between Sicily and Italy, and the latter a whirlpool, both of which were terrible to navigators; for unless a skilful pilot steered exactly between them, destruction of the vessel and crew was inevitable, either against the rocks, or in the gulf. It is said, however, that the latter was quite removed by an earthquake, which desolated Messina, in 1783. The poetical fiction is, that Scylla was a beautiful woman, changed by the envy of Circe into a monster; Scylla, in despair, threw herself into the sea, and was turned into a rock. Charybdis was a ravenous woman, changed by Jupiter into a gulph beneath the rock.

SEALS. The ancients endeavoured to prohibit the use of images of their idols on signs or seals; but in process of time this was little regarded. It became customary to have the figures of Egyptian and other deities—as well as of heroes, monsters, friends, ancestors, and even brutes—on their ring-seals. The use of them is of high antiquity. Jezebel, in 1 Kings xxi., seals the orders she sent for Naboth's death with the king's seal. Pliny tells us, at Rome they were become of absolute necessity, inasmuch that a testament was null without the testator's seal and the seals of seven witnesses. It was the custom in the middle ages for the sovereign to add greater sanction, when sealing his mandates, by embedding three hairs from his beard in the wax ; and there is still a charter of 1121 extant, which contains, in the execution clause, words recording that the king had confirmed it by placing three hairs from his beard in the seal.   The Etruscans sealed treaties with blood, and dough or paste has been used.   Wax is, however, the most usual substance, and the several colours which we know are white, yellow, red, green, black, blue, and mixed.

SEA TERMS. " Windward," from whence the wind blows ; " leeward," to which it blows ; " starboard," the right of the stern ; " larboard," the left ; " starboard helm," when you must go to the left ; but when to the right, instead of larboard helm, " helm a-port ;" " luff you may," go nearer to the wind ; " theis " (thus), you are near enough , " luff no near," you are too near the wind.   The tiller, the handle of the rudder , the capstan, the weigher of the anchor ; the buntlines, the ropes which move the body of the sail, the bunt being the body ; the bowlines, those which spread out the sails and make them swell ; ratlines, the rope ladder by which the sailors climb the shrouds ; the companion, the cabin-head ; reefs, the divisions by which the sails are contracted ; stunsails, additional sails spread for the purpose of catching all the wind possible ; the fore-mast, the front mast ; mainmast, the centre mast , mizen-mast, the stern mast , being pooped, having the stern beaten in by the sea , to belay a rope, to fasten it ; the sheets, a term for various ropes ; the halyards, ropes which extend the topsails ; the painter, the rope which fastens the boat to the vessel ; the " eight points of the compass," south, south and by east, south south-east, south-east and by east, south-east, east-south and by east, east south-east, east and by south-east ; and so on for the north, etc. The knowledge of these points is termed "knowing how to box the compass."

SEA-WATER. Some people account for sea-water being salt, that beds of salt are naturally deposited in the bottom of the ocean, and was intended by Providence to preserve the water from putrefaction; others consider that, as every river runs into the sea, they carry with them sufficient salt for that purpose (it being one of the principles in nature), and mixed in greater or less quantities, with every other substance ; and as no water runs out of the sea, but is only exhaled from it, no salt escapes in this way, rain-water being proved to be sweet, pure, and light.

SHAGREEN. Is a sort of grained leather prepared from the skin of the wild ass, chiefly used for watch and spectacle cases, etc. It is coloured red, green, black, or yellow, according to the taste of the manufacturer; and is chiefly brought from the states of Barbary, Constantinople, Poland, and Siberia.

SHAMROCK. Various opinions are given why the shamrock was made the emblem of Ireland. Some assert that the Irish people consider it the best and richest fodder for cattle, and that no other country could produce it but theirs. Others suppose that when St. Patrick, their patron saint, endeavoured to explain the mystery of the Trinity, and being unable to contend against the superstition of the age, he had recourse to a visible image ; he therefore took the shamrock, or trefoil, and made it emblematic of the divisibility of the Divinity into three distinct parts, united in one stem. (See *St. Patrick.*)

SHERIFF. A sheriff means a shire-reeve, or a governor of a shire or county ; that is, a gentleman nominated by the monarch to enforce a due observance of the laws in the county. His business is to execute the mandates of the sovereign, and all writs directed to him from the courts of law. He also empanels juries to bring causes and criminals for trial, and see that the sentences, both in law and justice, are properly executed. He appoints an under-sheriff, officers of court, constables, gaolers, etc.; and at the court of assize, when he waits on the judges, he has a number of men in rich liveries to attend on him.

SHILLING (Cutting off with). This had its origin with the ancient Romans, and was adopted to punish those children who were deficient in filial respect and duty. If the parent left any legacy, however small, he was considered "*compos mentis,*" or in his right mind ; but if he neglected to do this, the lawful heir could lay claim to his property as the next of kin. Hence arose the vulgar error of the necessity of leaving the heir a shilling, in order effectually to disinherit him. (See *Vulgar Errors.*)

SHIRES. The territorial divisions of England are not the consequences of a legislative act of any single governing body ; they are the effect of the ancient partition of the country among chiefs. The counties were their shires, or shares (for it is the same word) of territory. Thus Berkshire is a corruption of Beroc's share, the share of Beroc, a powerful chieftain.

SHOE (Beating with). This is a well-known chastise-

183

ment in Persia, and the shoe being shod with iron, and the blow given on the mouth, the punishment is severe. The shoe was always considered as vile, and never allowed to enter sacred or respected places ; and to be smitten with it, is to be subjected to the last ignominy. Paul was smitten on the mouth, by order of Ananias (Acts xxiii. 2).

SHOES. The ancient Jews wore shoes made of leather or wood; those of their soldiers were sometimes formed out of brass or iron. The Egyptians wore a shoe made of the papyrus. The Indians, the Chinese, and other nations wore shoes of silk, rushes, linen, wood, the bark of trees, iron or brass, and of gold and silver ; and luxury has sometimes covered them with precious stones. The Greeks and Romans wore shoes or boots of leather ; those of the Greeks generally reached to the middle of the leg. The Romans used two kinds of shoes—the *calceus*, which covered the whole foot, and was something like our shoe ; and the *solea*, or slipper, which covered only the sole of the foot, and was fastened with leather thongs. Black shoes were worn by citizens of ordinary rank, and white ones by women. Red shoes were put on by the chief magistrates of Rome on days of ceremony. In more recent times, this indispensible article of dress assumed the form of the jack boot, red heel, pointed toe, deerskin brogue, sandal, mocassin, etc. In Richard II.'s reign, Polish peaked, high-toed shoes, a yard long, fastened to the knees by silver chains, were in fashion ; in Henry VIII.'s time a shoe half a yard wide, slashed and padded like a small cushion.

SHREW. This word signified, anciently, any one perverse or obstinate of either sex. Shakespeare has,—

"By this reckoning *he* is more shrew than she "

Johnson, under "Shrewmouse," gives a curious conjecture which is worth repeating. Having quoted the Saxon root, he describes it as "a mouse of which the bite is generally supposed venomous, and to which vulgar tradition assigns such malignity, that she is said to lame the foot over which she runs. I am informed that all these reports are calumnious, and that her feet and teeth are equally harmless with those of any other little mouse. Our ancestors, however, looked on her with such terror, that they were supposed to have given her name to a scolding woman, whom for their venom they called a shrew."

SHROVE-TIDE. Shrove-tide, or Shrove Tuesday, is from the Anglo-Saxton *scrifan*, to confess, and signifies the time of confessing sins, for which purpose the day was anciently set apart by the Church of Rome, as a preparation for the austerities of Lent. This season was likewise called Feasting-tide, Fastens, and Fastmas. In some districts of the North, and in Ireland, it is still known by these titles. After the people had made confession, they were permitted to indulge in amusements of various kinds, but they were not permitted to partake of flesh meat : hence arose the custom of eating fritters and pancakes at Shrove-tide. The earliest day on which this Tuesday can fall in any year is February 3, the latest March 9.

SIGN MANUAL. When the sovereign was so ill as to be unable to write, a stamp was employed, as in the case of Henry VIII., 1547 ; James I , 1628 ; and George IV., May 29, 1830. Hence the signification.

SIGNATURE OF THE CROSS This is a mark which persons who are unable to write are required to make,

185

and this practice was formerly followed by kings and nobles. This signature is not, however, invariably a proof of ignorance. Anciently, the use of it was not confined to illiterate persons, for amongst the Saxons this mark, as an attestation of the good faith of the person signing, was required to be attached to the signature of those who could write, as well as to stand in the place of the signature of those who could not write. In those times, if a man could write, or even read, his knowledge was considered proof presumptive that he was in holy orders. The word *clericus*, or clerk, was synonymous with penman ; and the laity, or people,who were not clerks,did not feel any urgent necessity for the use of letters. The ancient use of the cross was therefore universal ; it was, indeed, the symbol of an oath, from its holy associations, and, generally, the mark. This explains the expression of "God save the mark," as a form of ejaculation ; and the phrase occurs three or four times in the plays of Shakespeare.

SIGNS. It was originally a custom to hang a bush of evergreens before houses of entertainment, from which circumstance arose the proverb, that " Good wine needs no bush," implying that where the best wine was sold, people were sure to resort. As these houses multiplied, different signs were necessary, many of which have the most ridiculous and absurd names. The sign of the Bag of Nails is derived from the Bacchanals; the Goat and Compasses, from " God encompasseth us," a favourite motto of Oliver Cromwell and his followers, who visited ale-houses ; the Bull and Mouth, from Boulogne Mouth, a common sign when England held that harbour in France ; the Swan with Two Necks. from two nicks, or marks. in their bills; as gentlemen used to mark or nick their swans, in order to know their own when they mixed with those of their neighbours ; the Belle Sauvage, from Mrs. Isabella or Bella Savage, who originally kept the house known by this name. (See *Chequers.*)

SILVER WEDDING DAY. This name is applied to the twenty-fifth anniversary of a marriage, and on this day it is customary to present the married pair with some *silver* token of remembrance. The custom prevails in some parts of northern Europe, where the festival of the twenty-fifth anniversary is called the "silver wedding," and that of the fiftieth the "golden wedding." The "siller marriage" of Aberdeenshire is altogether a different thing from the "silver wedding," being the same as the "pennie-brydal," or "penny wedding," which is a wedding where the guests contribute money.

SIRENS. These are described very fully in Homer's "Odyssey." They were two maidens who lived on an island in the ocean. They would sit close to the sea-shore, and sing with such power and melody that all who heard them were so charmed that they forgot home, friends, every thing that they loved, and hastened to these maidens, but as no food was found on the island, they would soon starve to death, and leave their bones to whiten on the shore.

SIRLOIN. The "roast beef of Old England" is celebrated throughout the world, and the most popular joint is the sirloin, from its having, it is said, been once actually knighted by Charles II., in one of his merryfrolics.*

* I fear the old story about Charles II. knighting a loin of beef,

SISTER ARTS. This term is generally applied to music, poetry, painting, and sculpture, although it must be admitted that other arts have proved of more benefit to mankind, such as writing, printing, etc.

SKATING. The origin of skating is unknown, but that the exercise was practised at an early period of the world's history is beyond dispute. There is mention made of the art in the ancient books of Norse mythology, and in feudal times the citizens of London, and elsewhere in England, were right glad when frost made solid ground of the watery highway, and with the leg bones of animals fastened under the soles of their feet, they sped over the ice, assisting themselves with a pointed stick—a support that would be scorned by modern skaters. In Northern Europe, the long and severe frosts of winter render skating not only a pastime but a necessity. The Dutch women, with baskets of eggs on their heads, skate to market over the smooth canal; ordinary citizens take their skates with them when they go out to business, and soldiers are sometimes taught to perform even military exercise in cumbrous skates. In England and France, skating is simply an amusement.

and thus giving origin to the word Sirloin, is but another vulgar error. In last year's exhibition at the Royal Academy, the story is, however, assumed to be true, and made the subject of a picture. But some years ago, the Rev. J. N. Simkinson, in his tale, "The Washingtons," quoted largely from the household books preserved at Althorp, in one of which, under the date 1623, is the following entry· "For a Sirloin . . . and a round of beef." In Nare's "Glossary" (edition, 1859), the following quotation is made from "The Abortive of an Idle Houre, 1620:" "One end of a sur loin of beefe called the buckler-piece."

You will perceive that the word "Surloin," is used before Charles II began his reign.   *H. J. Loaring.*

SKIN FLINT. The antiquity of certain proverbs is among the most striking singularities in the annals of the human mind. Abdalmaleck, one of the Khaliffs of the race of Omiades, was surnamed by way of sarcasm, Raschel Heigiarah, that is the skinner of a flint; and to this day we call an avaricious man a skin flint.

SKY. This term is applied to that region, or space, beyond the atmosphere, which surrounds our earth; or rather to that blue, beautiful, and infinite concavity which limits the power of vision with any obstructive body. The word itself has different meanings in different languages, such as the region of the clouds, shadow, space, the heaven, etc.; but, literally speaking, when we look up, on a clear, cloudless evening, and the eye wanders into unlimited space, it is imagined that we behold a vast and boundless object, beautifully studded with luminous bodies; but this is only ideal, and the seeming object is merely the extent of our optical faculties.

SLEEPS LIKE A TOP. This we say of a person completely under the influence of Morpheus; and we generally imagine the simile taken from the momentary pause of a peg-top or humming-top when its rotary motion is at its height. But it is no such thing, the word top is Italian. *Topo* in that language signifies a mouse; it is the generic name, and applied indiscriminately to the common mouse, field-mouse, and dormouse, from which the Italian proverb, " *Ei dorme come un topo,*" is derived—"He sleeps like a mouse."

SOUND AS A ROACH. St. Roche, or Roch, was the esteemed saint of persons afflicted with the plague. It is asserted he was healed of the plague of boils by a Divine communication. St. Roche's Day, in August, was formerly the general harvest-home day.

SOY Is the juice of a pod-bearing plant growing in Japan, called the *soja hispida* (the *j* should be pronounced as *y*). The plant grows to the height of four feet, its leaves are like the common kidney-bean. The seeds, termed *daikser*, in Japan, are used in soups, besides being consumed in other food three times a day.

SPERMACETI. An oily substance found in the head of the Cachalot whale. The method used in preparing it, is, to boil it over the fire, and pour it into moulds; this boiling is repeated till it becomes perfectly white and refined; it is then cut into flakes, and sold to the druggists. Spermaceti is frequently made into candles: the oil is used for lamps, and the refined part for asthmas and inward bruises.

SPICK AND SPAN NEW. This proverbial phrase is from *spica*, an ear of corn, says one writer; another, *spike* is a sort of nail, and *spawn* the chip of a boat; so that it is all one as to say, every chip and nail is new. But, correctly, it comes from *spike*, which signifies a nail, and a nail in measure is the sixteenth part of a yard; and *span*, which is in measure a quarter of a yard, or nine inches; and all that is meant by it, when applied to a new suit of clothes, is, that it has been just measured from the piece by the nail and span.

SPILLING SALT. An idea prevails that this is unlucky. This took its rise from one of the original paintings (in the Italian school) of the Last Supper, in which Judas Iscariot

190

is represented as having knocked over a salt-cellar This superstitious thought is still so prevalent, that when persons spill salt, they take a portion and throw ito ve r the left shoulder, for which custom no reason is assigned.

SPINNING. Prior to the year 1767, the mode of spinning was confined to the well-known domestic machine, called the *one-thread wheel;* and the manufacture of cloth was one of the humblest of our domestic arts, being confined chiefly to the fireside and cottage of the labouring poor of Lancashire. Subsequent improvements in machinery have imparted vigour and activity to cotton-spinning, and rendered it one of the most flourishing and important branches of our national industry. (See *Cotton* and *Knitting.*)

SPINSTER. In former ages, females were not allowed to marry till they had spun a regular set of bed furniture ; and till after their marriage they were called spinsters, which continues to the present day.

SPIRIT RAPPING. This is but an ancient theory enlarged and reduced to practice. Zeno and the Stoics supposed the soul to continue until the body was entirely putrefied and resolved into its first elements, but after that to be extinguished and vanish. In the meantime, while the body was consuming, it wandered all abroad, announcing things from afar and revealing secrets. The rapping is merely a mode of communication invented for the convenience of the rappers, and as a means of concealing an imposition which would be palpable if the spirits or their human familiars were to speak.

ST. CRISPIN Crispinus and Crispianus. two brothers,

were born at Rome ; whence they travelled to Soissons in France, about the year 303, to propagate the Christian religion. Being desirous of rendering themselves independent, they gained a subsistence by shoemaking It having been discovered that they had privately embraced the Christian faith, and endeavoured to make proselytes of the inhabitants, the governor of the town immediately ordered them to be beheaded, about 308. From this time, the shoemakers chose them for their tutelar saints.

ST. JOHN'S BREAD. The fruit of the carob-tree was supposed to have been eaten by St. John in the wilderness (see *Evangelist*), whence it was named St John's Bread. The peasants of France and Germany gather on St. John's day a species of the plant, St. John's Wort, and hang in their windows, as a charm against evil spirits.

ST. MARK'S DAY. The order of Knights of St. Mark, at Venice, under the protection of this evangelist, who is usually depicted with a winged lion by his side, was instituted in the year 737. The custom of sitting and watching in the church porch on the eve of this day, (25th April,) still exists in some parts of the north of England. The "witching time of night" is from eleven till one ; and the third year the watcher supposes that he sees the ghosts of those who are to die the next year pass by him into the church

ST. PATRICK (Order of) was instituted by George III., in 1782. It consists of the sovereign, grand master, and twenty-two knights. The insignia are The Star, inscribed with the motto, "*Quis separabit ?*" the collar of gold and the jewel suspended from a light blue ribbon. This Protestant saint died at an advanced age, and was buried in the cathedral city of Down. For some pious reason the Reformers left his name out of the calendar, but there is little likelihood of the day (17 March) being forgotten by the saint's adopted countrymen. (See *Shamrock.*)

ST. SWITHIN'S DAY. St. Swithin, or Swithum, was a bishop of Winchester, who died in 868. Being a wise man and a good Christian, he was not ambitious of the vain distinction of being buried in the chancel of the minster, but wished to be laid where the rain of heaven might wet his grave. He was accordingly interred in the minster yard; but the monks, who were more worldly-minded, resolved to remove the body into the choir of the church. This was to have been done on the fifteenth of July, but it rained then, and for forty days after, so violently, that they abandoned the design. Hence the expression, that if it rain on St. Swithin's day, it will rain for forty days after successively.

STANDARDS. The earliest account of them is in the Bible. It is evident they were in use among the Hebrews in the time of Moses, in order to distinguish the tribes. The standard of Benjamin was a wolf; and that of Ephraim, a steer.

STAR (Falling) is a little fiery meteor which is often witnessed on a clear evening. It is merely a small cloud, containing a sort of gaseous exhalation in its centre, which, by growing continually hot, is spontaneously kindled, and the fire runs through the cloud till the vapour is exhausted; but being free from electric matter, no noise is occasioned by the ignition. It burns gradually, and has the appearance of a sky-rocket in the air.

STAR OF INDIA. This order was instituted by Queen Victoria in 1861. It consists of the sovereign, grand master, and twenty-five knights, together with such extra and honorary knights as the sovereign may be pleased to appoint. The insignia are, the star, inscribed with the motto, "Heaven's Light our Guide," the collar of gold; and the badge, suspended from a light-blue ribbon, with a narrow white stripe toward either edge.

STENOGRAPHY. This mode of writing was known to the Greeks; and Plutarch, in his life of Cato, informs us that the celebrated speech of that patriot relating to Catiline's conspiracy, was taken in shorthand. Cicero, at that time consul, placed *notarii,* or shorthand writers, in different parts of the senate house to preserve the speech. We are also further informed, that Titus Vespasian was remarkable for the rapidity with which he wrote shorthand. He not only applied it to purposes of business, but of diversion; it was his custom to get his amanuenses together, and entertain himself with trying which of them could write the fastest.

STENTORIAN VOICE. In the army which marche against ancient Troy, was a Grecian warrior named Stentor, whose voice was so loud that it was equal to the combined voices of fifty men; hence the term, "Stentorian Voice."

STERLING.· The following extract from Camden will explain the origin and use of this word. "In the time of king Richard I., monie coined in the east parts of Germanie began to be of especiall request in England for the puritie

194

thereof, and was called *Easterling* monie, as all the inhabitants of those parts were called *Easterlings*, and shortly after some of that countrie, skilful in mint matters and alloies, were sent for into this realme to bring the coins to perfection, which since that time were called of them *Sterling*, for *Easterling*."

STOCK-BROKERS.   Stock-jobbing, or broking, was contemporaneous with the creation of our national debt, in 1695, and gave rise to that class of money-dealers who have the exclusive *entrée* to the Stock Exchange.

STORMY PETREL.   The petrel keeps in the wake of the ship, a few yards from the rudder, disporting in the eddies, and literally "picking up a living" from the surface of the wave.   It is probable that, like other sea birds, its home is some desolate rock in the waste of ocean.   In their rapid flight—being *palmiped*, or web-footed—they skim over the surface of the waves, and even "walk on the water."   Hence, in fact, the name *Petrel*, from the Italian diminutive, *Pietrillo*, or *Little Peter*, alluding to the fact recorded of St. Peter in St. Matthew's Gospel.   (See *Chickens*.)

SUGAR.   It is asserted that the use of sugar was known to the ancient Hebrews.   The first distinct notice of the sugar cane is in the account of the expedition undertaken by Nearchus down the Indus, in the time of Alexander. It appears to have been cultivated in Sicily as early as 1166, at which place there was also a mill for grinding it.   From Sicily the cane was transported by the Portuguese to Madeira in 1420, and to St. Domingo by Columbus in 1493. In 1641, it was transplanted from Brazil to Barbadoes, and thence to our other West India islands. The boiling and baking of sugars was first practised in Europe about 1420 ; and the art of refining sugar, and of forming it into cones, was communicated by a Venetian in 1550. (See *Loaf Sugar.*) ·

SUPREME BEING. This is spelt with four letters in almost every language, namely :—It is in Latin, *Deus ;* French, *Dieu ;* Greek, *Theos* (Θεός); German, *Gott ;* Scandinavian, *Odin ;* Swedish, *Codd ;* Hebrew, *Adon ;* Syrian, *Adad ;* Persian, *Syra ;* Tartarian, *Idga ;* Spanish, *Dies ;* East Indian, *Esgi,* or *Zeni ;* Turkish, *Addi ;* Egyptian, *Aumn,* or *Zeut ;* Japanese, *Zain ;* Peruvian, *Liau ;* Wallachian, *Zene ;* Etrurian, *Chur ;* Irish, *Dieh ;* and in Arabian, *Alfa.*

SURGEON (Sergeant). The appointment of sergeant surgeon is one of great antiquity. One of the duties is to be in attendance on the king when he ventures to battle ; and the earliest record of this appears when John of Ardern, in 1349, accompanied Edward III. to the battle of Crecy. The office of sergeant surgeon was not, however, confirmed until 1461, when William Hobbys was appointed, with a salary of forty marks yearly. There were several perquisites attached, and he was, moreover, the twelfth person in rank, and took precedence accordingly. Abroad, they were treated with distinguished consideration, as, on the death of a sovereign, they were beheaded and buried with him.

SURNAMES. Their origin is not only curious, but very interesting, there being scarcely any instrument or object in creation which has not been chosen as a subject for a surname. They were first used in 1102, and became common in 1200. Many names are so far corrupted, that it is rather difficult to trace them. For instance, we have the surname of Death, which is derived from De-Ath, a noble family in France; also the surname Devil, which is derived from De Ville, another French family of note; we have also Moon, Star, Cloud, Heaven, Hedger, Ditcher, and every trade, employment, place, office, dignity, vegetable, utensil, fish, colour; and in short, everything in the whole system of nature. Originally, people's surnames had only reference to the qualities which they possessed; and this plan was adopted in consequence of the increase of population; but taking the Bible for our guide, the surname was added to distinguish successive generations. Thus we read of Isaiah, the son of Amos; Caleb, the son of Jephunneh, etc.; but on the introduction of Christianity, about the date above mentioned, other names preceded the family names, such as Matthew, Mark, Luke, etc. (See *Names.*)

SWORD OF DAMOCLES. The origin of the simile is as follows:—About the year 400 B.C., the ancient city of Syracuse was ruled by Dionysius, commonly called the "Tyrant;" but the Greeks applied this term to one who usurped any power, without regard to the manner in which he ruled. If he was mild and wise in exercising his power, they considered him as no less a tyrant. Among his courtiers was a man named Damocles, who fawned about Dionysius, and seemed to be infatuated with the grandeur and pomp of royalty. He was continually speaking of the happiness which he thought was the constant portion of kings. To undeceive him, Dionysius prepared a magnificent feast for him, and surrounded him with all the luxury which a monarch could command. Damocles was delighted, but in the midst of his pleasure, happening to cast his eyes upward, he was horrified at the sight of a sharp sword suspended over his head by a single horsehair. He compre-. hended the meaning, which was, that the position of a usurper was by no means secure, but in continual danger of some impending calamity.

SYMBOLS AND NUMBERS. Ten, as the radix of numerical computation, has been raised to the dignity it now holds by the circumstance of its expressing the number of man's fingers. A *digit* is a finger's breadth ; an *inch*, the length of the thumb ; a *nail*, from the tip of the middle joint of the longest finger ; a *palm*, the breadth of four fingers ; a *hand*, the fist, with the thumb uppermost; a *span*, the space between tips of thumb and finger extended to the utmost , a *foot*, that of a man ; a cubit, from the elbow to the end of the longest finger ; a *yard*, the girth of a man's body ; a *step*, when each foot advances alternately ; a *pace*, two steps ; a *fathom*, width to which a man's arms and hands can extend.

T.

TABERNACLES (Feast of) A Jewish festival of eight days' continuance, in the seventh month, which corresponds with our October, during which time they left their habitations, and dwelt in booths, or tents, in commemoration of their dwelling forty years in tabernacles in the wilderness. This feast was kept up with great rejoicings ; at the close of their vintage and harvest, they carried in their hands branches of palm, olive, willow, and myrtle, tied with gold and silver cords ; and once every day they went round the altar of the temple, crying " Hosanna ! O Lord ! send us prosperity." The priest then went to the pool of Siloam, and filled a golden vessel with water, which he mixed with wine, and poured on the altar as a libation, the people singing, "With joy shall ye draw water from the wells of salvation."

TAILORS (Nine). The expression of "Nine tailors make a man," is an old English vulgar adage, and had its origin from a poor beggar, who craved charity at a tailor's shop, where there were nine men at work, each of whom contributed a trifle, and gave him the total. The beggar fell on his knees, and thanked them, saying they had made a man of him.

TAKE THIS AND BE THRIFTY. In observance of a fanciful derivation of Egglesfield, the founder of Queen's College, Oxford, from *aigulle*, needle, and *fil*, thread, it has been customary for the bursar of the college to give to each student, on New Year's Day, a needle and thread, saying at the time, "Take this and be thrifty." A needle and thread have long been emblems of thrift; and Holinshed tells us, that when Henry (V.) Prince of Wales repaired to court, to clear himself of the imputation of dissolute indolence, he wore "a gown of blue satin, full of oilet (eyelet) holes, and at every hole a needle hanging by a silken thread," in token of his careful remembrance of collegiate discipline.

TALLIES. (See *Taxes.*)

TALMUD. This is the literature of the Jews for a thousand years, including all the elements of Babylonian, Persian, Greek, and Roman culture. Though not written till after the New Testament, it is virtually intermediate

199

between it and the Old Testament. It tells us all that the Jews thought and did during the most important period of their history; and it becomes the great commentary by which we may explain the New Testament. It is an undesigned support to the system of the latter, all the stronger because independent.

TANTALIZING. This word is derived from Tantalus, an ancient king of Corinth, who one day gave a feast to the gods, at which he served up the body of his son Pelops. The gods were greatly incensed at being invited to such a banquet, and all refused to partake of it, except the goddess Ceres, who had recently lost her daughter Proserpine, which so distracted her, that before she was aware, she had eaten a shoulder of the ill-fated boy. Jupiter proposed that the remaining parts should be put into a cauldron. This was done, and Mercury drew out the boy alive and whole all but the shoulder, and an ivory one was made to supply the deficiency; and this shoulder possessed the power of removing every disorder and healing all complaints by its touch. Tantalus was punished for his cruelty, by being placed up to his chin in water, where he was tormented with thirst, and when he attempted to drink, the water would avoid him. Above his head grew delicious fruits, but when he stretched forth his hand to take them, a breeze would waft them out of his reach. This was certainly provoking enough, and our word "tantalize" we can understand all the better, having heard its origin.

TARRING AND FEATHERING. This, it seems, is an English invention. One of Richard Cœur de Lion's ordinances for seamen was, "that if any man was taken with

200

theft or pickery, and thereof convicted, he should have his head polled, and hot pitch poured upon his pate, and upon that the feathers of some pillow or cushion shaken aloft, that he might thereby be known 'for a thief, and at the next arrival of the ships to any land, be put forth of the company to seek his adventures without all hope of return to his fellowes."

TAXES. This word is derived from the Latin word, *tallia*, or *tallium*, which in the ancient signification meant a piece of wood, squared and cut into two parts, on each of which they used to mark what was due and owing between debtor and creditor; from thence it came to signify a tribute paid by the vassal to the lord, on any important occasion, the particular payments whereof were marked on these pieces of wood, one part being held by the tenant, the other by the lord. In French it is *taille*, which originally signified no more than a section or cutting, from the verb *tailler*, to cut; but afterwards it came to signify a tax, or subsidy : all which words come from the pure Latin word *talea*, a cut stick, or tally. From whence is derived our law Latin word *tallagium*, or rather *talliagium*, which signifies in our law any sort of tax whatsoever.

TEA. The tea-plant is a small evergreen shrub, a native of China, Japan, and other countries. About the year 1591, the Dutch East India Company brought into Europe the dried leaves of this shrub, and taught the method of producing an agreeable beverage by infusing them in boiling water. This seems to have been so much approved of, that by the year 1660, it became a favourite drink in coffee-houses ; and the Government, taking advantage of this circumstance, imposed a duty of eightpence a gallon on the liquor sold in those places. At this period, the price of tea is stated to have been about sixty shillings per pound ; and being thus too dear to be bought by the general consumer in the leaf, its infusion was ordinarily purchased ready-made, at so much per pint, quart, or gallon. The first importation of tea by the English East India Company was in 1669, when two canisters, weighing 143 lbs., were forwarded to England by the resident merchants at Canton. About the year 1720 tea was generally drank by the middle classes of society.

TEA BRANDS. The meaning of the names given to some of our tea brands may not be generally known. " Hyson " means " before the rains," that is early in the spring ; hence it is often called " Young Hyson." " Hyson Skin " is composed of the refuse of other kinds, the native term for which is " tea skins." " Bohea " is the name of the hills in the region in which it is collected. " Pecoe," or " Pecco," means white hairs, the down of tender leaves. " Pouchong " means folded plant ; " Souchong," small plant. "Twankey " is the name of a small river in the region from whence it is brought. " Congo " is from a term signifying labour, from the care required in its preparation.

TEARS (Bottled). In some of the mourning assemblies of the Persians, it is the custom for a priest to go about to each person at the height of his grief, with a piece of cotton in his hand, with which he carefully collects the falling tears, and which he then squeezes into a bottle, preserving them with the greatest caution. This practically illustrates that passage in Psalm lvi. 8, " Put thou my tears into thy bottle." Some persons believe, that in the agony of death,

202

when all medicines have failed, a drop of tears so collected, put into the mouth of a dying man, has been known to revive him ; and it is for such use that they are collected.

TEETOTAL. The simple facts are, that when the question of revising the old temperance pledge, so as to exclude all intoxicating liquors, was under consideration in Preston, a working man, of the name of Richard Turner, applied to the proposal, not a cant word, but one long in use as an idiomatic local expression, the term "Teetotal." He had probably heard and uttered it hundreds of times before, in the sense of "completely," "absolutely, without any exception," or, as we sometimes say, "out-and-out." The formation of the word is clear enough, the first syllable "tee" being the mere duplicate of the initial " t " of total, for the sake of greater emphasis and force. Its application to total abstinence from inebriating liquors was accidental ; and the use of it by Richard Turner would probably have escaped observation had he not, through a habit of stammering, drawn the attention of the people to the distinction he was wishing to convey.

TEETH (Spite of his). King John once fined a Jew ten thousand marks, and on his refusing to pay, he ordered one of his teeth to be drawn daily till he consented. The Jew lost seven, and then paid the fine. Hence arose the expression, " In spite of his teeth."

TELEGRAM. When and where this word was first used as a heading for telegraphic intelligence, is easily ascertained. On the 27th of April, 1852, in the *Daily American Telegraph*, published in Washington, the editor thus introduces the word :—"Telegraph, means to write from a dis-

203

tance ; Telegram, the writing itself, executed from a distance. Monogram, logogram, etc., are words formed upon the same analogy and in good acceptation. Hence telegram is the appropriate heading of a telegraphic despatch." (See *Electric Telegraph.*)

TENTERDEN STEEPLE (and Goodwin Sands). It is reported that those quicksands were once firm land, in the possession, and named after Earl Goodwin ; and that the Bishop of Rochester, employing the revenue assigned to maintain the banks against the encroachment of the sea, upon the building and endowing Tenterden church, the sea overwhelmed the land ; whereupon grew the Kentish proverb, that Tenterden steeple is the cause of Goodwin Sands. (See *Goodwin Sands.*)

TEXTS. The custom of taking a text as the basis of a sermon or lecture, is said to have originated about the time of Ezra, who, accompanied by several Levites, in a public congregation of men and women, ascended a pulpit, opened the book of the law, and after addressing a prayer to the Deity, to which the people said, "Amen," "read in the law of God distinctly, gave the sense, and caused them to understand the reading." Previous to the time of Ezra (457 years B.C.), the patriarchs delivered in public assemblies either prophecies or moral instruction for the edification of the people ; and it was not until the return of the Jews from the Babylonian captivity, during which time they had almost lost the language in which the Pentateuch was written, that it became necessary to explain as well as to read the Scriptures to them—a practice adopted by Ezra, and since universally followed. In later times (Acts xv. 21), the book of Moses was read in the synagogue every Sabbath-day. To

204

this custom our Saviour conformed, and in the synagogue, one Sabbath-day, read a passage from the prophet Isaiah; then closing the book, returned it to the priest, and preached from the text. This custom, which now prevails all over the Christian world, was interrupted in the dark ages, when the "Ethics" of Aristotle were read in many churches on Sunday, instead of the Holy Scriptures.

THE MASTER'S EYE MAKES THE HORSE FAT. The answers of Perses and Libys are worth recording. The former, being asked what was the best thing to make a horse fat, answered, "The eye of the master:" the other being questioned, what was the best manure? replied "The master's footsteps." There is also the story of Gellius: A fat man riding upon a lean horse, was asked, how it came to pass that himself was so fat, and his horse so lean, replied, "Because I feed myself, but my servant feeds my horse."

THISTLE. The most current opinion as to the thistle being chosen as the emblem of Scotland, is, that during the invasion of the Danes, it was thought an act of cowardice to attack an enemy in the dark. The invaders, availing themselves of this idea, determined to assail their opponents at night, and, to prevent a knowledge of their approach, they walked barefooted. One of the Danes happening, however, to tread on a very large thistle which abounds in that country, he instinctively cried out from the acute pain: this alarmed the Scots, who instantly took to their arms, and defeated the enemy with great slaughter; from which circumstance the thistle was adopted as the national emblem.

THISTLE (Order of the) is said to have been instituted by king Achaius of Scotland, in 819 (the history of the Scoto-Irish from 503 to 1843 is very obscure); but its origin must be ascribed to James V., in 1534. It was revived by James II., in 1687, and re-established by queen Anne, in 1703. The badges are the star, of silver, inscribed with the motto : " *Nemo me impune lacessit* ;" the jewel, or figure of St. Andrew, suspended from a green ribbon ; and the collar, of gold.

THREE GRACES. These were mythological charac-ters, comprising three young and beautiful sisters, said to be attendants of Venus. Their names were Aglaia, meaning *splendour ;* Euphrosyne, meaning *joy ;* and Thalia, meaning *pleasure.* It was the belief among the ancient Grecians that the graces presided over the banquet, the dance, and all descriptions of festivities. They are usually represented with their arms twined affectionately together.

THUMB SCREW. This was an inhuman instrument, commonly used in the first stages of torture by the Spanish Inquisition. It was in use in England also. The Rev. William Carstairs was the last who suffered by it before the Privy Council, to make him divulge secrets entrusted to him, which he firmly resisted. After the revolution in 1688, the thumb-screw was given him as a present by the council. King William, it is said, expressed a desire to see it, and tried it on, bidding the doctor to turn the screw; but at the third turn he cried out, " Hold ! hold ! doctor ; another turn would make *me* confess anything."

TIDES. Homer is the earliest profane writer who speaks of the tides. Posidonius, of Apanea, accounted for the tides by the motion of the moon 79 B. C. ; and Cæsar

206

speaks of them in his book of the "Gallic War." The theory of the tides was first satisfactorily explained by Kepler, 1598; but the honour of a complete elucidation of them was reserved for Sir Isaac Newton, about 1683.

TIME (taken by Forelock). In heathen mythology, the painters represented Time under the figure of a man, holding a scythe in one hand, and an hour-glass in the other; he is quite bald, except one little spot in the forehead, where there is a small tuft of hair. Hence, in order to prosper in the world, and lose no time in frivolous pursuits, we are enjoined to take time by the forelock.

TIME (Jewish division of). The Jews adopted a plan of subdividing time into four vigils, or watches, which was, in some degree, practised by the Romans. The first began at sunrise, or six in the morning; the second at nine; the third at noon; and the fourth at three in the afternoon. The night watches, also, were observed in every three successive hours. The Greeks reckoned their first quarter from sunset to midnight; the second, from midnight to sunrise; the third, or morning watch, from sunrise to noon; and the fourth, from noon to sunset. The Romans, however, had their watches from midnight to cock-crowing; from cock-crowing to dawn; from dawn to mid-day; from that time to vesper or evening twilight; and thence to midnight.

TOFANA (Aqua). This is the name of a poisonous liquid, which excited extraordinary attention in Naples at the end of the seventeenth century. Tofana, a Sicilian woman, seems to have invented it. After she had murdered many hundred men, she was strangled. The drink is described as transparent, tasteless water, of which five or six drops were fatal—producing death slowly, without pain, inflammation, convulsion, or fever.

TOGA (Highland). The Highlander still wears the adaptation of the toga, fastened by the Roman brooch; the Phrygian cap is on his head, and the Roman crossed garters are represented in his chequered stockings. Thomas Rawlinson, about 1728, introduced the pheliebeg, or short kilt worn in the Highlands.

TOMBSTONES. It is certain that tombstones were only used subsequent to the introduction of Christianity, as we read in the Old Testament that people were buried in caves, under trees, and in other convenient places. The Egyptian pyramids (see *Wonders of the World*), were the burying places of the monarchs, and mausoleums were used for the same purposes. The first account we have of tombstones was about the year 590, when Pope Gregory authorized the relatives of the deceased to erect tablets, tombstones, etc., to their memory; that on reading the inscription, they might be induced to offer up prayers for the welfare of their souls; but this was attended with a heavy expense, and added greatly to the revenues of the church. Prior to this, there were no churchyards in England, nor any regular burying-places; nor did they become common till the latter end of the seventh century. (See *Burying Grounds.*)

TOMBOY. Verstegan gives the following origin of this word, applied to romping girls :—" *Tumbe*, to dance ; *tumbod*, danced ; hereof we yet call a wench that skippeth or leapeth like a boy, a *tomboy :* our name also of *tumbling* cometh from hence."

208

TONTINES. Lorenzo Tonti, a Neapolitan (who died in the Bastile after seven years' imprisonment), invented the system of tontines, or loans given for life annuities, with benefit of survivorship, in 1653. They were first set on foot in Paris to reconcile the people to Cardinal Mazarin's government, by amusing them with hope of becoming suddenly rich. A Mr. Jennings was an original subscriber for a £100 share in a tontine company; and being the last survivor of the shareholders, his share produced him £3000 per annum. He died worth £2,115,244, aged 103 years, on June 19th, 1798.

TOWER (Locking up the). This is an ancient, curious, and stately ceremony. A few minutes before the clock strikes the hour of eleven—on Tuesdays and Fridays, twelve—the head warder, clothed in a long red cloak, bearing a huge bunch of keys, and attended by a brother warder carrying a lantern, appears in front of the main guard-house, and loudly calls out, " Escort—Keys." The sergeant of the guard, with five or six men, then turn out and follow him to the "spur," or outer gate ; each sentry challenging as they pass his post, "Who goes there ?"— " Keys." The gates being carefully locked and barred, the procession returns, the sentries exacting the same explanation and receiving the same answer as before. Arrived once more in front of the main guard-house, the sentry there gives a loud stamp with his foot, and asks, "Who goes there ?"—" Keys." "What keys ?"—" Queen Victoria's keys." "Advance, Queen Victoria's keys, and all's well." The yeoman porter, or head warder, then exclaims, " God bless Queen Victoria ! " The main-guard respond, " Amen." The officer on duty gives the word, " Present arms !" the firelocks rattle; the officer kisses the hilt of his sword; the escort fall in among their companions; and the yeoman porter marches across the parade alone to deposit the keys in the lieutenant's lodgings. The ceremony over, not only is all egress and ingress totally precluded, but even within the walls no one can stir without being furnished with the countersign.

TRAIN-BANDS were a kind of volunteer corps, formed in connection with the London Artillery Company, at the time when the invasion of England was threatened by the Spanish Armada. They were first called into existence in 1585. The train-bands were again called together at the breaking out of the civil wars, and incorporated with the City Artillery Company at the Restoration.

TRAJECTORY is the curve a body describes in space when projected. Applied to rifle-shooting, it indicates the course of the bullet, which, instead of being a straight line, forms a complete curve, which augments more in proportion as the distance from the muzzle increases.

TRANSPORTATION was first inflicted as a punishment in the time of Queen Elizabeth, when it was enacted that all rogues dangerous to the people should be banished. But it was not much resorted to till the reign of Charles II., when persons found guilty of offences entitled to the benefit of clergy, were transported to the British settlements in North America, not as slaves but servants; being bound by indenture to their masters for seven years, the last three of which they were entitled to wages. During the reign of Henry VIII., 72,000 convicts were executed, for almost every offence known on the criminal calendar.

TREES. There are numerous remarkable trees amongst which may be named the bread-fruit tree of Ceylon, the fruit of which is baked and eaten as. we eat bread, and is equally good and nutritious. In Barbuta, near Maracarbo, South America, is a tree, which by piercing the trunk, produces beautiful milk, with which the inhabitants feed their children. In the interior of Africa is a tree which produces excellent butter! It resembles the American oak, and its fruit, from which the butter is prepared, is not unlike the olive. The great traveller, Park, declared that the flavour surpassed any made in England from cow's milk, and it will keep a whole year. At Sierra Leone is the cream-fruit tree; but this, although agreeable to the taste, is as viscous as birdlime. At Table Bay, near the Cape of Good Hope, is a small tree, or shrub, the berries of which make excellent candles. It is also found in the Azores and America. The vegetable tallow-tree also grows in Sumatra; and the bark of a tree in China produces beautiful soap. The talypot tree in Ceylon grows to the height of 100 feet, the leaf of which is so large, that it will cover nearly twenty people like an umbrella. The banian-tree is the most wonderful of all, as it never dies, and is constantly extending, for as the branches shoot downwards, they take root, and thus produce other trees, whose branches in like manner extend onwards, and resemble large oaks, the fruit of which is much like rich scarlet figs, and is a luxurious subsistence to monkeys and birds of every description. Numerous other astonishing specimens might be named, which our limits prevent describing.

TROPICS AND ZONES. Tropic is derived from a

Greek word, which means turn, or conversion, as being the utmost limits of the sun's declination north or south; so that when the sun arrives at either of these points, he begins to return towards the equator. Zones are so called from a Greek word implying a girdle, being broad spaces encircling the earth. There are five of these swathes, which are named according to the different degrees of heat and cold, viz. :—one torrid, two temperate, and two frigid zones.

TURNPIKES. These were erected in 1267, and a grant of one penny for each wagon passing through a manor imposed. The derivation of the word is—That in early times it was the custom to fasten a pike or spearhead loosely to the top of a post, in order to prevent the intrusion of travellers not duly authorized to pass, the turning round of this post, presenting a pike on every side, gave rise to the name " Turn-pike."

TWELFTH DAY. It appears this originated with the Greeks and Romans, who had a custom of drawing lots for a king and queen on this day, in allusion, it is supposed, to the offerings made by the wise men to the Saviour of the world, from an idea that the eastern magi were kings. In fact, the French term it " The Feast of Kings;" but the Greeks, about this season of the year, drew lots with beans, and, like kings, exercised some temporal authority. It was formerly practised in our universities by the division of a cake, into which a bean, piece of coin, or ring, had been placed, and he or she who chanced to obtain these was saluted as king or queen. The cakes originally used, called twelfth cakes, were made of flour, honey, pepper and ginger, but are now composed of plums and other rich ingredients, and frosted over with sugar. On this day, it has been usual for the monarch, or his chamberlain, to offer gold, frankincense, and myrrh, at the chapel royal. (See *Baddeley Night.*)

TYRIAN SHIPS. These were very remarkable, and frequently made of cedar, the benches of ivory, the finest embroidered Egyptian linens were used for sails, and their canopies were of scarlet and purple silk.

U.

UMBRELLA. The umbrella, or parasol, is by no means a recent invention; and the earliest mention we find of this most useful article is by Aristophanes, who flourished about 407 B.C. Parasols were frequently given as presents. And then, as now, a common mark of attention was for a gentleman to carry the parasol when walking with a lady. The men did not carry them in those days, on account of its being considered effeminate. Frequently, the Roman and Grecian ladies employed slaves, generally women, to carry their umbrellas.

UNDER LEASE. A person is said to make an under-lease, or to under-let, when, being a tenant for years, he re-lets his holding for part of the term he has in it; or being a tenant from year to year, he lets again to another tenant of the same kind.

UNIFORMS. The adoption of a distinguishing style and colour of dress for bodies of men, is due to Charles VII. of France, who, about the middle of the fifteenth century, having formed a regiment of cavalry, obliged them to wear the livery of the captain of the corps to which they belonged, that the men might be known in action, or discovered, if guilty of irregularities, for which purpose their coats were ornamented with appropriate colours; and hence proceeded the system of wearing uniforms, which has since been established among European troops. In this country, the soldiers or retainers belonging to particular barons, wore the badges of their respective employers. In the reign of Henry VIII., white was the prevailing national uniform. Under Elizabeth, dark green or russet distinguished the infantry, while scarlet cloaks were worn by the cavalry. A naval uniform came into use at the commencement of the eighteenth century.

UZ. The land of Uz comprehended that rich and fertile country which surrounds Damascus, and a large portion of Arabia Petræa. Ophir included those countries on the eastern part of China and Japan. The garden of Eden was situated north of the Persian Gulf, between the rivers Tigris and Euphrates.

V.

VALENTINE'S DAY. The custom of sending valentines on the 14th of February, took its rise from a superstitious heathen habit, when youths used to send their favourites a kind of love-letter in honour of one of their goddesses, as they supposed that on this day birds choose their mates. St. Valentine was a holy priest, "a valiant and noble knight of God," who suffered martyrdom in the persecution under the Roman emperor Claudius II., in the year 270. Some people suppose that on this day the patron saints were chosen in the papal countries. Charles, Duke of Orleans, who was made prisoner at the battle of Agincourt (1415), was the first to write poetical epistles or communications in the shape of valentines. His example was soon followed, and not only male, but female suitors (or at least admirers), adopted this covert mode of declaring their affection. It was formerly the custom for a lover to send some substantial or tangible proof of affection to the object of his regard (and this practice is being restored). Pepys, in his "Diary," boasts that he sent to his wife, when she was staying at Sir W. Batten's, "half a dozen pairs of gloves, and a pair of silk stockings and garters for her valentines." There were frequently mottoes attached to such gifts of a complimentary kind. The *minnesingers* of Germany never neglected the periodical opportunity of making or declaring love through the instrumentality of a valentine.

VEGETABLES. Almost all our corn, vegetables, and flowers, were brought from foreign countries. Rye and wheat are indigenous to Tartary and Siberia; rice was first brought from Ethiopia; buck-wheat from Asia; potatoes from Brazil; gourds and melons from Astracan; cauliflowers from Cyprus; asparagus from Asia; cresses from Crete; parsley from Egypt; shallots from Siberia, etc. Jasmine came from the East Indies; the elder-tree from Persia; tulip from Cappadocia; daffodil, carnation, and pink from Italy; lily from Syria; tuberose from Java and Ceylon; and the aster from China. In short, nearly every choice garden-flower now cultivated is of foreign origin, and in general from a warmer climate than ours.

VIGILS. They were originally instituted on the days of dedication of the churches, or on those saints' days to whom

215

these edifices were devoted, and commenced on the evenings preceding those days. They must have been of early origin, as St. John alluded to them (chap. x., verse 22).

VIPER WOMAN. The subjoined extract is from the vestry-book of the parish of Nailsea, Somerset :—" 1762. At a Vestry Meeting held ye 14th day of January, it is agreed that the Viper Woman do make a trial on John Lovell, at a Guinea per week." There is evidence from another entry in the overseers' accounts, that John Lovell was a pauper. Twenty-eight years before the date of the entry on the Nailsea register, William Oliver and his wife, of Bath, had discovered an effectual remedy for the bite of a viper. Their experiment was first tested at Windsor, in May, 1734, before Dr. Durham and Dr. Waterland ; and again on June 1, same year before several members of the Royal Society, of which an account was drawn up by Cromwell Mortimer, M.D., and printed in the " Philosophical Trans-actions." The remedy was the common oil of olives, better known by the name of salad oil, and was no doubt turned to a profitable account by other non-professional practitioners in other parts of the country.

VINEGAR DRINKING. In some countries, parti-cularly in the West Indies, people are obliged to use a great deal of vinegar ; and the Roman soldiers used to take it in their marches. People in the East used to dip their bread in it, and eat it as one of their chief articles of refreshment, and this custom still prevails in France and Italy. It is supposed that when the Roman soldier offered it to the Saviour, it was some which he used for his own drinking : there was a sort, however, which was too potent for use until diluted.

In some countries they mix oil with it, particularly in Algiers, where they even indulge their miserable captives with a small portion of oil to the vinegar, which they allow with their bread. The above explains the scriptural expression, " They gave Him vinegar to drink."

VINEGAR (River of). This is a river or small stream at Popayan, in South America, called Rio Vinegre. It rises in a very high chain of mountains, and after a subterraneous course of some miles, it reappears, and forms a magnificent cascade three hundred feet in height. A person standing near is speedily driven off by a fine shower of acid water, which irritates the eyes, and causes great pain.

VISCOUNT—or Vicount (*Vice Comes*) signifies as much as sheriff ; between which two words there seems to be no other difference, but that the one comes from the Normans, the other from our Saxon ancestors. It is a degree of nobility next to an earl, which, Camden says, is an old name of office, but a new one of dignity, never heard of amongst us till Henry VI., in the eighteenth year of his reign, created John, Lord Beaumont, Viscount Beaumont. It seems, however, as a title of honour, to be far more ancient in other countries.

VULGATE. The Vulgate is a very ancient translation of the Bible, which was translated from the Greek of the Septuagint. It is the only one acknowledged by the Romish Church to be authentic.

VIOLIN. The antiquity of the violin has long been a subject of dispute : it is generally supposed that the ancients were unacquainted with any instruments played

217

with a bow. The general opinion appears to be that the violin was invented by the Italians in the tenth century, at which time it was called the rebec, and had but three strings; when the fourth string was added is not known. During the reign of Cromwell, the use of the violin was superseded by that of the viol, a rude instrument with six strings; but at the Restoration, Charles II. established at court a regular band of violin players; hence the instrument became popular, and has remained so ever since. Cremona, in Italy, was once famous for the manufacture of violins, and has given its name to the most highly-prized descriptions.

W.

WALES (Prince of). When the Saxons made themselves masters of South Britain, most of the Ancient Britons retired to Wales, where they defended themselves with the utmost bravery against the invaders; and afterwards made many vigorous attempts to maintain their liberties against the encroachments of the kings of England. Edward I., however, subdued the whole country, and annexed it to the crown of England. Perceiving that the Welsh were not entirely reconciled to this revolution, he sent his queen to be delivered in Caernarvon Castle. There a son was born, whom Edward very politically styled " Prince of Wales," which title the heir to the crown of Great Britain has borne ever since.

WALL-PAPER was introduced into Europe to supply the place of the ancient tapestry with which houses were hung. The Chinese have used it for that purpose from a very early day. The English claim to have introduced it

218

into Europe; but the French deny their claim, and assert that paper-hangings were first made in Rouen, as early as 1620 or 1630, by one Francois. At present, France is more largely engaged in the manufacture of wall-paper than any other country, and its productions stand first in the market for beauty and excellence.

WANDERING JEW. This strange personage is supposed to have been Calaphilus, Pontius Pilate's porter, who, when they were dragging Jesus out of the door of the judgment-hall, struck him on the back, saying, " Go faster, Jesus! go faster; why dost thou linger?" Upon which Jesus looked on him with a frown, and said, " I am indeed going; but thou shalt tarry till I come." Soon after, he was converted, and took the name of Joseph. He lives for ever; but at the end of every hundred years he falls into a fit or trance, upon which, when he recovers, he returns to the same state of youth he was in when our Saviour suffered, being about thirty years of age; always preserves the utmost gravity of deportment, was never seen to smile, and perfectly remembers the death and resurrection of Christ.

WAR INSTRUMENTS. Most warlike instruments took their names from the places where they were made : thus, bayonets were invented at Bayonne, in France; pistol from Pistoya, a city of Tuscany; chevaux-de-frise (*a Frieseland horse*) is derived from Frieseland, where it was invented. A sword is often called a Toledo, from Toledo, in Spain, which has long been famous for sword blades. Bilboa also implies a rapier, or sword, because at Bilboa, likewise in Spain, instruments of steel were in the highest perfection.

A broadsword took the name of Ferrara, from Ferrara, in Italy, or from Andica de Ferrara, a celebrated aitificer of that place, who served the Scotch Highlanders with their sword blades.

WATERSPOUTS. This phenomenon usually occurs when a whirlwind happens at sea. The water, for the same reason that it rises in a pump, or forms a fountain in an exhausted receiver, rises in the vacuum of the whirl to the height of thirty or thirty-three feet, forming a pillar of water in the air, widest at the top ; and the conversion of some of the upper part of the pillar into vapour, by heat which originally occasioned the whirlwind, often forms a dense cloud. Waterspouts are observed of all sizes, from the thickness of a finger to twenty-five feet in diameter, and, at their junction with the ocean, the ocean appears to boil. If a large waterspout were to break over a ship, the vessel would either be destroyed or would sustain very grievous damage ; when, therefore, they appear to be coming very near, the sailors avert the danger by firing a shot against the water, and thus dissipating them. When not disturbed, they generally break about the middle.

WATER SUPPLY. London was first supplied with water by means of leaden pipes, in 1237. It was procured from springs at Tyburn, which, in 1285, were made to communicate with a large conduit at Cheapside. In 1613, Sir Hugh Myddelton finished his canal (New River) for supplying London with water, and soon afterwards wooden pipes were laid in the streets, with small leaden pipes for conveying the water into private houses ; but water-carriers were still attached to Aldgate Pump in the time of Queen Anne.

WAYZGOOSE. The celebration by most of the London printing-houses and newspaper establishments of the annual "wayzgoose," is of very ancient date, probably as old as the time when William Caxton practised typography in a house now called the Almonry, near the western door of Westminster Abbey, from 1476 to 1491, where he died. Randle Holme, a writer in 1688, says, "It is customary to make every year new paper windows in Bartholomew-tide (August 24), at which time the master printers make them a feast called a wayzgoose, to which is invited the *corrector, founder, smith, ink maker,* etc., who all open their purses and give to the workmen to spend in the tavern or alehouse after the feast, from which time they begin to work by candlelight."

WEATHER SIGNS. When the wind sets in the north, we have a right to expect cold weather, as it blows from the north frozen zone, or colder countries than ours, without much sea. The south wind is generally attended with heat, because it comes to us from the torrid zone, or hotter countries than ours. The east wind is the driest, because it comes over the great continent of Asia and Europe, where there are few seas. The west wind is generally attended with rain, because it blows over the great Atlantic Ocean, whence a great quantity of vapours arise. Whether clear or cloudy—a rosy sky at sunset presages fine weather; a red sky in the morning, bad weather, or much wind (perhaps rain); a grey sky in the morning, fine weather; a high dawn, wind; a low dawn, fair weather. A high dawn is when the first indications of daylight are seen above a bank of clouds. A low dawn is when the day breaks on or near the horizon, the first streaks of light being very low down. Soft-looking or delicate clouds foretell fine weather, with moderate or light breezes; hard-edged, oily-looking clouds, wind. A dark, gloomy blue sky is windy, but a light, bright blue sky indicates fine weather. A bright yellow sky at sunset presages wind; a pale yellow, wet. After fine clear weather, the first signs in the sky of a coming change are usually light streaks, curls, whisps, or mottled patches of white distant cloud. Dew is an indication of fine weather, and so is fog.

WEATHERCOCKS ON STEEPLES. Churches were originally built without steeples, but as soon as these were added—in the eighth century—they were surmounted by a vane, which was made to resemble a cock, the emblem of watchfulness. Hence the term, weathercocks.

WHERE THE SHOE PINCHES. The following is said to be the origin of the well-known saying, " Nobody knows where the shoe pinches but he who wears it :"—A Roman being about to repudiate his wife, among a variety of other questions was asked by her enraged kinsman, "Is not your wife a sensible woman? is she not handsome?" In answer to which, slipping off his shoe, he held it up, asking them, "Is not this shoe a very handsome one? is it not quite new? is it not extremely well made? How, then, is it that you can't tell me where it pinches?"

WHIG AND TORY. Whig was a name of reproach given by the court party to their antagonists for resembling the principles of the whiggs, or fanatical conventicles in Scotland; and tory was given by the country party to that of the court, comparing them to the *tories*, or popish robbers in Ireland. They formerly were called whiggs, from Whiggamors, a name given to the Scots in the south-west; who, for want of corn in that quarter, used annually to repair to Leith to buy stores that came from the north, and all who drove were called whiggamores, or whiggs, from the term wiggam, in driving their horses. In the year 1638, the Presbyterian ministers incited an insurrection against the court, and marched with the people to Edinburgh; this was called the whiggamor's inroad, and after this, all that opposed the administration in Scotland were called whigs, and from hence the term was adopted in England. Politically, whig means "liberal," and "tory" an advocate for royal power.

WHIPPING BOY. English princes were originally induced to learn, by having a whipping boy placed with them; and so lately as the reign of Edward VI. it was customary for the Prince of Wales to have one, a boy of noble birth, who waited on him, and was always whipped if the prince were idle; this boy would therefore teaze the prince to learn, by crying, "O pray, save me from a whipping."

WHIT-SUNDAY. This corresponds with the Jewish feast of Pentecost, so called from being celebrated fifty days after the Passover. The Christians called it Whit, or White-Sunday, as being the day on which their converts should dress in pure white to receive the sacrament. It is also kept in commemoration of the visible appearance of cloven tongues, which rested on the apostles, and by which they were endued with miraculous power.

WHITTINGTON AND HIS CAT. This nursery story has been well known in Persia for centuries. It was

223

imported into Europe much about the same time as others, of which Boccaccio, Sachetti, etc., availed themselves. There is an old Hungarian tradition to the same effect; both were, doubtless, derived from the same source. In these instances the story is, of course, unconnected with any English worthy; and it is believed that it was not applied to Sir Richard Whittington until late in the reign of Elizabeth, when some such man as Richard Johnson, author of the "Seven Champions," or Thomas Delouy, author of the "Six Yeomen of the West," converted the tale to their own purposes. (See *Cinderella*).

WILDERNESS. This word is derived from three different languages. *Wild* from the Dutch; *der* from the British *dur*, meaning water; and *ness* from a Saxon word, signifying a termination of a tract of land.

WISE MEN OF GOTHAM. These worthies, whose name has almost passed into a household word, thus acquired their unenviable celebrity:—King John, intending to pass through this place towards Nottingham, was prevented by the inhabitants; they no doubt apprehending, by a vulgar error still prevalent, that the ground over which a king should pass would ever after be public road (see "Vulgar Errors"). The king, incensed at their proceedings, sent from his court soon afterwards some of his servants to inquire the reason for such incivility, in order that he might punish them. The Gothamites, hearing of the approach of the king's servants, thought of an expedient to turn away the king's displeasure; and so they shammed more stupidity than really belonged to them. When the messengers arrived at Gotham, they found some of the inhabitants engaged in endeavouring to drown an eel in a pool of water; some were employed in dragging carts upon a large barn to shade the wood from the sun; or lifting horses into lofts to eat hay; and others were engaged in hedging in a cuckoo which had perched in a bush. In short, they were all employed in some ridiculous task or other, which convinced the king's servants that Gotham was a village of fools—a reputation it has ever since maintained.

WOOLSACK. The term, as applied to the Lord Chancellor's seat in the House of Lords, originated in the circumstance, that wool, being once the staple commodity of the country, it was thought fitting that so high a dignitary as the Lord Chancellor should be seated thereon. The "woolsack" of the present day is simply a covered comfortable cushion.

WORLD (Four Quarters of). *Europe* derives its name from Europa, daughter of Agenor, king of Phœnicia, who was represented to have been carried hither by Jupiter. *Asia* received its name from Asia, the wife of Prometheus, and daughter of Oceanus. *Africa* is derived from Ophir, grandson of Abraham, or, as some authors suppose, from the Hebrew *pheric*, an ear of corn, from its fertility. *America* is (unjustly) so called from Americus Vesputius, who gave it his own name after the death of Columbus, the first who discovered it (1492), and named it Columbia.

WORLD (how Peopled). According to the best historical accounts, Noah is supposed to have peopled the vast Chinese empire; Japheth peopled Europe, and the northwest parts of Asia; Ham peopled Africa, and carried thither the curse of his father, Noah, which is fully exemplified in the degraded state of this unfortunate people to the present day ; Shem peopled the southern parts of Asia. It is not known by whom America was peopled, but it is generally supposed that some of Noah's descendants emigrated thither, and spread themselves over this immense continent.

WORLD (Wonders of). These were seven in number. The *First* was a colossal statue of brass at Rhodes, which was dedicated to the sun. It was twelve years in making, and cost 300 talents (or about £97,000 of our money). It was seventy cubits in height, and stood directly across the harbour. Its thumbs were so large, that a man could not clasp one of them with both his arms, and its legs were spread out to such a distance, that ships of large size could sail between them. In its left hand it held a light-house, for the direction of mariners ; and in its right, a dart, apparently ready to be discharged at any intruder. Fifty years after its erection, it was thrown down by an earth-quake; and about nine centuries subsequently, the old metal was purchased by a Jew, who loaded 900 camels with it. *Second :* the pyramids of Egypt, three of which still remain. The first has a square base, 660 feet each way, and is 500 feet high. It is made of great stones, the least of which is thirty feet in height. It took 360,000 men twenty years to complete it. The other two are a little smaller, and attract the admiration of the spectator. Some suppose they were built by the Israelites, during their captivity ; but this opinion cannot be correct, as we read that they were employed in making bricks. *Third :* the walls of the city of Babylon, built by queen Semiramis. They formed an exact square, were sixty miles in circumference, 200 feet in height, and fifty in breadth, so that six chariots could travel upon them abreast. *Fourth :* the temple of Diana, at Ephesus, which

226

was a work of the greatest magnificence. The riches within were immense; and the goddess was worshipped with great solemnity. It took 220 years in its completion, *though all Asia was employed!* It was supported by 127 pillars of beautiful Parian marble, each of a single shaft, and raised by as many *kings.* Each pillar was sixty feet in height, thirty-seven of them being engraven. The beams and doors were made of cedar, and the rest of the timber was cypress. The image of the goddess was made of ebony : it was burnt by Erostratus, an obscure individual, 110 years after, on the same day that Alexander the Great was born. *Fifth:* the royal palace of Cyrus, king of Media. It was built by Memnon, who was as prodigal in expense as he was skilful in building. It is asserted that he actually cemented the stones with gold ! Some are inclined to give the preference to the temple of Solomon, at Jerusalem, as a superior edifice. *Sixth:* the statue of Jupiter Olympus, in the city of Olympia. It was of prodigious size, made of ivory, and carved with the greatest art by Phidias, a noted sculptor. *Seventh:* the mausoleum, or sepulchre of Mausolus, King of Caria, built by his queen, Artemisia, of the most beautiful marble. The workmanship was splendid in the extreme; it was sixty-three feet in length, 400 in circumference, and thirty-five in height, surrounded by thirty-six columns of the most superb workmanship. This has been acknowledged by some, as one of the seven wonders, whilst others think that the light-house of Alexandria ought to have the preference. This was a tower of white marble, nearly 400 feet in height, with magnificent galleries, and mirrors of enormous size. On the top was an immense lantern, with a light constantly burning, so that ships could perceive it at a distance of a hundred miles.

WORST ART. In Lincolnshire, the peasantry, on hearing any bad news, exclaim, " Worst art !" This is also said in Yorkshire and Scotland ; but it ought to be expressed "waes t' 'eart," and is a contraction of " wae 's the heart ; " the speaker meaning that his heart is woe (or, as pronounced, *wae*), or sorry, at the bad news communicated.

X.

XX. Certain ales are called XX (Double X) and XXX (Treble X), because, originally, all ale or beer sold at or above 10*s.* per barrel, was reckoned to be strong, and was therefore subject to a higher duty. The cask which contained this strong beer was then first marked with an X, signifying *ten ;* hence the present quack-like denominations, as above.

Y.

YANKEE DOODLE. This American tune is probably of Dutch origin, and it is asserted by some authorities that a tune strongly resembling it is still a harvest song in Holland. It is known to have been famous in England in the reign of Charles I., when it used to be sung to such words as—

> " Lucy Locket lost her pocket,
> Kitty Fisher found it ;
> Nothing in it, nothing in it,
> But the binding round it."

YEOMAN. A yeoman, in the common acceptation of the word, means a gentleman farmer ; originally it meant a yewman, from his bearing the bow in battle, which was generally made of yew, from which we may infer that a

228

yeoman was of equal consequence with an esquire, or shield-bearer. We have now yeomen of the crown, guard, chamber, etc.—all persons of some rank in society. In some languages, however, it signifies boy, servant, knave, etc. In this sense it might have been used in the patriarchal forms of society, where the younger people waited on the elders.

YEW TREES. Some suppose that these trees were originally planted in churchyards on account of their being evergreen, and furnishing branches for the decoration of churches at Christmas ; others think it was to prevent cattle from being turned into consecrated ground : this tree, possessing noxious qualities, would poison them if they happened to eat it. It is also asserted that bees will not live where yew-trees abound.

YULE CAKE. A little image, called the yule dough, or yule cake, was formerly presented by bakers to their customers on the anniversary of the Nativity. This practice is obsolete, and in its stead we now have, before breakfast, something more beautiful, in the words—

> "God bless you, merry gentlemen,
> Let nothing you dismay,
> Remember Christ our Saviour
> Was born on Christmas-day."

Z.

ZODIAC. The zodiac is a great circle on the globe, extending about eight degrees on each side of the equator, in which the sun performs its apparent revolution, and from which it never departs. It derives its name from a Greek word, signifying an animal, or, as some authors imagine,—life ; because the planets were formerly supposed to have great influence on animal life. The former, however, is the most authenticated opinion, as each of the signs, in the early ages, represented some animal, Libra being incorporated with Virgo and Scorpio. The zodiac is divided into twelve portions, called signs, which signs are denominated constellations, and are descriptive of the seasons of the year, or sun's path.

ZODIAC (Signs of). *Aries,* the first, is represented by a ram; the sun entered this sign about March 21st, when lambs were principally brought forth. *Taurus,* the bull, implied that the sun entered this sign when calves were brought forth. *Gemini,* or the twins, was originally represented under the figure of two kids; the sun entered this sign when goats brought forth their young, generally twins, at a birth. *Cancer,* the fourth sign, was represented by a crab—an animal which always walks sideways (?) or backwards, the sun being then in its most northerly declination, touching the tropic of Cancer, and beginning to retrograde, or go back, towards the equator. *Leo,* the fifth sign, was portrayed by the figure of a lion, in consequence of the intense heat which prevails at this season, and which the Egyptian astronomers compared to the ferocity of the lions in the wilds of Abyssinia and Ethiopia, when it was observed they were more formidable than at any other season; and when they sought the waters of the Nile, etc., to quench their raging thirst, they were doubly ferocious and destructive. *Virgo,* the sixth sign, was represented by a woman holding an ear of corn in her hand, emblematic of a gleaner; the sun entered this sign about the time of harvest. *Libra,* or the balance, was made emblematic of a pair of scales, equally poised, indicating that the days and nights were then equal all over the world. *Scorpio*, the eighth sign, was displayed under the figure of a scorpion—the most venomous animal in creation ; they therefore chose this, being emblematic of the sickly season, which was, and still is, the most unhealthy portion of the year. *Sagittarius*, or the archer, was represented under the figure of a centaur— that is, a fabulous animal, the fore part being like that of a man holding a bow and arrow in the act of shooting, the hind parts those of a horse; and when the sun entered this sign, November 22nd, the hunting season commenced. *Capricornus*, the goat, was very aptly chosen. The sun, being then in its most southerly declination, touching the tropic of Capricorn, begins again to ascend towards the equator, the goat being an animal which delights in climbing up mountains, rocks, and very steep ascents. *Aquarius*, or the water-bearer, was represented by a man holding a pitcher, and pouring forth a constant stream of water, as it was at this period that their rainy season commenced. *Pisces*, the twelfth sign, was displayed under the figure of two fishes tied together, in token of their being taken ; reminding people that this was the most proper season for fishing, and that the quality of the fish was better than at any other part of the year.

Butler & Tanner, The Selwood Printing Works, Frome, and London.

L'ᒑ

1⁰⁄₂

Lightning Source UK Ltd.
Milton Keynes UK
UKOW06n1358091215

264345UK00001B/47/P